每天读一点英文

Everyday English Snack

那些美好而忧伤的记忆

The beautiful and dolorous Memory

章华◎编译

与美国人同步阅读的英语丛书

——美国英语教师协会推荐——

陕西师范大学出版社

图书在版编目（CIP）数据

那些美好而忧伤的记忆：英汉对照/章华编译. —西安：
陕西师范大学出版社,2009.7
（每天读一点英文）
ISBN 978-7-5613-4728-7

Ⅰ.那… Ⅱ.章… Ⅲ.①英语—汉语—对照读物
②故事—作品集—世界 Ⅳ. H319.4:I

中国版本图书馆 CIP 数据核字（2009）第 106403 号

图书代号：SK9N0663

上架建议：英语学习

那些美好而忧伤的记忆（温情卷）

作　　者：章　华
责任编辑：周　宏
特约编辑：辛　艳　刘宇圣
封面设计：张丽娜
版式设计：风　筝
出版发行：**陕西师范大学出版社**
　　　　　（西安市陕西师大 120 信箱　邮编：710062）
印　　刷：北京嘉业印刷厂
开　　本：880×1230　1/32
字　　数：200 千字
印　　张：7
版　　次：2009 年 7 月第一版
印　　次：2012 年 1 月第八次印刷
ISBN 978-7-5613-4728-7
定　　价：21.80 元

目录
CONTENTS

First love，forever love
曾有一个人，爱我如生命

I wish someone were waiting for me somewhere
我希望有人在什么地方等我

爱和微笑，人生的**芳醇**

love and smile, the sweetest wine of life

Paving a Brilliant Way
铺就辉煌之路

· Barack Obama ·

Tonight is a particular honor for me because, let's face it, my presence on this stage is pretty unlikely. My father was a foreign student, born and raised in a small village in Kenya. He grew up **herding** goats, went to school in a tin-roof shack. His father, my grandfather, was a cook, a domestic servant to the British.

But my grandfather had larger dreams for his son. Through hard work and **perseverance** my father got a scholarship to study in a magical place: America, that shone as a **beacon** of freedom and opportunity to so many who had come before.

While studying here, my father met my mother. She was born in a town on the other side of the world, in Kansas. Her father worked on oil rigs and farms through most of the Depression. The day after Pearl Harbor, my grandfather signed up for duty, joined Patton's army, marched across Europe. Back home, my grandmother raised a baby and went to work on a bomber **assembly** line. After the war, they studied on the GI Bill, bought a house through FHA, and later moved west, all the way to

Hawaii, in search of opportunity.

And they, too, had big dreams for their daughter, a common dream, born of two **continents**. My parents shared not only an improbable love, they shared an abiding faith in the possibilities of this nation.

They would give me an African name, Barack, or "blessed," believing that in a tolerant America your name is no **barrier** to success. They imagined me going to the best schools in the land, even though they weren't rich, because in a generous America you don't have to be rich to achieve your potential. They are both passed away now. *Yet, I know that, on this night, they look down on me with great pride.*

爱和微笑，人生的芳醇

巴拉克·奥巴马

对我而言，今晚是特别荣耀的时刻。的确，从现实来看，我今天能现身在这个舞台上，简直就是不可能的事。我的父亲是一位外籍学生，在肯尼亚的小村庄出生、长大。他从小以羊为伴，在一间铁皮屋学校接受教育。他的父亲，也就是我的祖父，是英国人的家仆，担任厨师的工作。

但祖父对儿子怀抱着更远大的梦想。因此，靠着艰苦的努力和坚强的意志力，父亲获得了奖学金，在一个充满魔法的地方学习，那就是美国，这里闪烁着自由与机会的光芒，照亮了许多之前来到这里的人。

父亲在这里读书时，遇见了母亲。她出生在世界另一端的堪萨斯州的一个小镇。在大萧条时期，她的父亲，也就是我的外祖父，大部分时候在从事石油钻井的工作，闲时也务农。在珍珠港事件后的第二天，外祖父自愿入伍，投入巴顿将军旗下，远征整个欧洲。在家乡，我的外祖母边抚养孩子，边到轰炸机装配线上去工作。战后，他们利用美国退伍军人权利法案的资助继续深造，并通过联邦住宅管理局买了一栋房子。之后，为了寻找新的机会，他们迁往西部，就这样一路来到了夏威夷。

而他们对女儿同样也怀抱着远大的梦想。是的！一个共同的梦想，却诞生在两个洲。我的双亲不仅都拥有一份不同寻常的爱，也都怀抱着同样不变的信念——他们相信在这个国度里，没有不可能的事。

他们为我取了一个非洲式的名字巴拉克，意思是受祝福，他们相信，在兼容并蓄的美国，名字绝对不会是成功的障碍。尽管他们并不富裕，但却期望我能去这个国家最好的学校学习，因为在有容乃大的美国，你不一定要多富裕才能发挥你的潜能。他们现在都过世了，但我知道，就在今晚，他们正骄傲地俯瞰着我。

Practising

& Exercise

核心单词

herd [hə:d] *n.* 畜群；牧群 *v.* 放牧

perseverance [ˌpə:si'viərəns] *n.* 坚持不懈；坚忍不拔

beacon ['bi:kən] *n.* 烽火台灯塔；信号浮标 *v.* 明亮，指引

assembly [ə'sembli] *n.* 与会者；集合

continent ['kɔntinənt] *n.* 大陆，大洲 *adj.* 自制的，克制的

barrier ['bæriə] *n.* 障碍物；路障，栅栏

实用句型

Yet，I know that，on this night，they look down on me with great pride.

但我知道，就在今晚，他们正骄傲地俯瞰着我。

① on this night 在这里是插入语，其位置灵活，常常用逗号或破折号与其他成分隔开。

② look down on 轻视，类似的表达还有 look forward to 盼望；look back on 回顾，回头看；look ahead 考虑到将来等固定搭配。

翻译行不行

1. 两人之间逐渐产生了友情。(grow up)

....

2. 当"禁止吸烟"的指示灯亮时，请您熄灭香烟。(sign up)

....

3. 他妻子生病了，得去找医生。(in search of)

....

A Glass of Milk
一杯牛奶的温暖

• Betty Stantey •

One day, a poor boy who was trying to pay his way through school by selling goods door to door found that he only had one **dime** left. *He was hungry so he decided to beg for a meal at the next house.*

However, he lost his **nerve** when a lovely young woman opened the door. Instead of a meal he asked for a drink of water. She thought he looked hungry so she brought him a large glass of milk. He drank it slowly, and then asked, "How much do I **owe** you?"

"You don't owe me anything," she replied. "Mother has taught me never to accept pay for a kindness." He said, "Then I thank you from the bottom of my heart." As Howard Kelly left that house, he not only felt stronger **physically**, but it also increased his faith in God and the human race. He was about to give up and quit before this point.

Years later the young woman became **critically** ill. The local doctors were baffled. They finally sent her to the big city, where specialists can be called in to study her rare disease. Dr. Howard Kelly, now famous, was called in for the **consultation**. When he heard the name of the town she came from, a strange light filled his eyes. Immediately, he rose and went down through the hospital hall into her room.

Dressed in his doctor's **gown** he went in to see her. He recognized her at once. He went back to the consultation room and determined to do his best to save her life. From that day on, he gave special attention to her case.

After a long struggle, the battle was won. Dr. Kelly requested the business office to pass the final bill to him for **approval**. He looked at it and then wrote something on the side. The bill was sent to her room. She was afraid to open it because she was positive that it would take the rest of her life to pay it off. Finally she looked, and the note on the side of the bill caught her attention. She read these words...

"Paid in full with a glass of milk."

(Signed) Dr. Howard Kelly

Tears of joy flooded her eyes as she prayed silently: "Thank You, God. Your love has spread through human hearts and hands."

贝蒂·斯坦利

一天，一个贫穷的小男孩为了攒够学费正挨家挨户地推销商品。肚子饿得咕咕直响，可他摸遍全身，却只找到一角钱。于是他决定向下一户人家讨口饭吃。

　　然而，当一位年轻的美丽女子打开房门的时候，这个小男孩却有点不知所措了。他没有要饭，只乞求给他一口水喝。可她看出男孩肚子很饿，于是就倒了一大杯牛奶给他。男孩慢慢地喝完牛奶，问道："我应该付多少钱？"

　　年轻女子微笑着回答："一分钱也不用付。我妈妈教导我，施以爱心，不图回报。"男孩说："那么，就请接受我由衷的感谢吧！"说完，他就离开了这户人家。此时的他不仅浑身是劲儿，而且更加相信上帝和整个人类。而在这之前，他都感到万念俱灰了。

　　很多年之后，那位女子得了一种罕见的重病，当地医生对此束手无策。最后，她被转到大城市医治，并请来专家会诊。大名鼎鼎的霍华德·凯利医生也参加了医疗方案的制定。当他听到病人来的那个城镇的名字时，一个奇怪的念头闪过脑际。他马上起身直奔她的病房。

　　身穿白大褂的凯利医生来到病房，一眼就认出了恩人。回到会诊室后，他决心一定要竭尽所能来治好她的病。从那天起，他就特别关照这个对自己有恩的病人。

　　经过艰苦的努力，手术成功了。凯利医生要求把医药费用通知单送到他那里，他看了一下，便在通知单的旁边签了字。当医药费用通知单送到她的病房时，她不敢看。因为她确信，治病的费用一定非常昂贵，恐怕她下半辈子也难以还清了。最后，她还是鼓起勇气，翻开了药费通知单，旁边的一行小字引起了她的注意，她不禁轻声读了出来：

　　"医药费已付：一杯牛奶。"

　　（签名）霍华德·凯利医生

　　喜悦的泪水溢出了她的眼睛，她默默地祈祷："谢谢你，上帝，你的爱已通过人类的心灵和双手在传播。"

核心单词

dime [daim] *n.* 一角硬币

nerve [nə:v] *n.* 忧虑，焦躁；勇敢

owe [əu] *v.* 欠（债）；应该把……归功于

physically ['fizik(ə)li] *adv.* 身体上；实际上；完全地

critically ['kritikəli] *adv.* 批判性地；苛求地；危急地；严重地

consultation [ˌkɔnsəl'teiʃne] *n.* 咨询；商议；参考；参阅

gown [gaunk] *n.* 女礼服，（妇女穿的）长礼服；手术衣

approval [ə'pru:vəl] *n.* 批准；认可；赞成；同意

实用句型

He was hungry so he decided to beg for a meal at the next house.

他很饿于是他决定向下一户人家讨口饭吃。

①so 在这里引导因果状语从句。

②decide to 决定做，类似的表达还有 decide on 考虑后决定等固定搭配。

翻译行不行

1. 我替你去开会吧！（instead of）

....

2. 我出生在波士顿，但是大部分时间在费城。（come from）

....

3. 在付清贷款后，我们会有更多钱花。（pay off）

....

The Difference a Teacher Can Make
老师改变了男孩的人生

• Anonymous •

Steve, a twelve-year-old boy with alcoholic parents, was about to be lost forever, by the U.S. education system. **Remarkably**, he could read, yet, in spite of his reading skills, Steve was failing. He had been failing since first grade, as he was passed on from grade to grade. Steve was a big boy, looking more like a teenager than a twelve year old, yet, Steve went unnoticed...until Miss White.

Miss White was a smiling, young, beautiful redhead, and Steve was in love! For the first time in his young life, he couldn't take his eyes off his teacher ; yet, still he failed. He never did his homework, and he was always in trouble with Miss White. His heart would break under her **sharp** words, and when he was punished for failing to turn in his homework, he felt just miserable! Still, he did not study.

In the middle of the first semester of school, the **entire** seventh grade was tested for basic skills. Steve hurried through his tests, and continued to dream of other things, as the day wore on. His heart was not in school, but in the woods, where he often escaped alone, trying to shut out the sights, sounds and smells of his alcoholic home. No one checked on him to see if he was safe. No one knew he was gone, because no one was sober enough to care. Oddly, Steve never missed a day of school.

One day, Miss White's **impatient** voice broke into his daydreams.

"Steve!" Startled, he turned to look at her.

"Pay attention!"

Steve locked his gaze on Miss White with adolescent adoration, as she began to go over the test results for the seventh grade.

"You all did pretty well," she told the class, "except for one boy, and it breaks my heart to tell you this, but..." She **hesitated**, pinning Steve to his seat with a sharp stare, her eyes searching his face.

"The smartest boy in the seventh grade is failing my class!"

She just stared at Steve, as the class spun around for a good look. Steve dropped his eyes and carefully examined his fingertips.

After that, it was war! Steve still wouldn't do his homework. Even as the punishments became more **severe**, he remained stubborn.

"Just try it! ONE WEEK!" He was unmoved.

"You're smart enough! You'll see a change!" Nothing fazed him.

"Give yourself a chance! Don't give up on your life!" Nothing.

"Steve! Please! I care about you!"

Wow! Suddenly, Steve got it!! Someone cared about him? Someone, totally unattainable and perfect, CARED ABOUT HIM?!

Steve went home from school, thoughtful, that afternoon. Walking into the house, he took one look around. Both parents were passed out, in various stages of undress, and the stench was overpowering! He, quickly, gathered up his camping gear, a jar of peanut butter, a loaf of bread, a bottle of water, and this time...his schoolbooks. Grim faced and determined, he headed for the woods.

The following Monday he arrived at school on time, and he waited for Miss White to enter the classroom. She walked in, all sparkle and smiles! God, she was beautiful! He yearned for her smile to turn on him. It did not.

Miss White, immediately, gave a quiz on the weekend homework. Steve hurried through the test, and was the first to hand in his paper. With a look of surprise, Miss White took his paper. Obviously puzzled, she began to look it over. Steve walked back to his desk, his heart pounding within his chest. *As he sat down, he couldn't resist another look at the lovely woman.*

Miss White's face was in total shock! She glanced up at Steve, then down, then up. Suddenly, her face broke into a radiant smile. The smartest boy in the seventh grade had just passed his first test!

From that moment nothing was the same for Steve. Life at home remained the same, but life still changed. He discovered that not only could he learn, but he was good at it! He discovered that he could understand and **retain** knowledge, and that he could translate the things he learned into his own life. Steve began to excel! And he continued this course throughout his school life.

After high-school Steve enlisted in the Navy, and he had a successful **military** career. During that time, he met the love of his life, he raised a family, and he graduated from college Magna Cum Laude. During his Naval career, he inspired many young people, who without him, might not have believed in themselves. Steve began a second career after the Navy, and he continues to inspire others, as an adjunct professor in a nearby college.

Miss White left a great **legacy**. She saved one boy who has changed many lives. I know, because I am the love of his life.

You see, it's simple, really. A change took place within the heart of one boy, all because of one teacher, who cared.

佚　名

史蒂夫是一个 12 岁的小男孩，父母嗜酒成性，他面临着辍学的危险。显然，他会阅读，只是成绩总不尽如人意。从一年级到现在，年年如此。史蒂夫个子高大，看上去似乎比同龄的孩子要大得多。可他一直都被人忽视，直到怀特小姐的出现。

怀特小姐总是面带笑容，她年轻、还有一头亮丽的红头发。史蒂夫就喜欢她这种类型的，生平第一次。他无法将视线从老师身上移开，可是他的成绩还是不及格。他从不写作业，总是给怀特小姐添麻烦。她刻薄的言辞让他心碎，每当因没有完成作业而受罚时，他都非常痛苦，但他还是不学习。

第一学期期中，整个七年级都要进行基础技能测验。史蒂夫草草地将测验应付完，便继续幻想其他的事，一天天就这样过去了。他的心根本不在学校，而是在树林中。他经常独自躲藏在那里，以期避开酒鬼之家的吵闹声和令人作呕的气味。所有的人都无暇顾及他，没有人关心他是否安全，也没人知道他已经离开。奇怪的是，即便如此，史蒂夫却从没旷过一天课。

一天，怀特小姐不耐烦的声音把他从白日梦中惊醒了。

"史蒂夫！"他震惊地转过头看着她。

"不要开小差！"

怀特小姐公布七年级的测验结果时，史蒂夫用青春期男孩特有的那种爱慕的眼光盯着她。

"你们都考得不错，"她对学生们说，"除了一个男生，这令我很伤心，但是……"她犹豫了，犀利的目光锁定在史蒂夫身上，盯着他。

"我们七年级最聪明的学生，竟然没及格！"

她紧盯着史蒂夫，全班同学都转过头看着他。史蒂夫羞愧地低着头，盯着指尖。

此后，"战争"仍在继续！史蒂夫还是不愿写作业。即便惩罚再严厉，他也依然我行我素。

"努力试一下！坚持一周也好啊！"可他就是无动于衷。

"你很聪明！如果你努力一定会有可喜的变化！"没有什么话语可以打动他。

"给自己一个机会！不要轻言放弃。"仍无济于事。

"史蒂夫，求你了，我那么关心你！"

哦！史蒂夫突然恍然大悟！真的有人关心他？简直不可思议，竟然有人关心他？！

那天下午，史蒂夫满腹思绪地回家了。进了家门，他扫视了一下屋内，看到父母裸露着身子睡着了。屋内臭气熏天，简直让人无法忍受。他快速找齐露营装备：一瓶花生酱，一块面包，一瓶水，这次他还把课本带上了。他坚定地走向了树林。

紧接着的那个周一早上，他按时来到学校，期待着怀特小姐步入教室。她面带微笑神采飞扬地走进来了。天哪！她真是太美了！他希望看到她对他微笑，但她没有。

怀特小姐突然决定测试周末的家庭作业。史蒂夫很快就做完了，并第一个递交了答卷。怀特小姐满脸惊奇地接过他的卷子，她批阅试卷时的疑惑溢于言表。史蒂夫回到座位上，心怦怦地狂跳不止。坐下之后，他情不自禁地又瞄了一眼这位漂亮的女子。

怀特小姐脸上满是震惊的神情，她瞟了一眼史蒂夫，又低下头去，然后又再次抬起头来。突然，她脸上绽放出灿烂的笑容。七年级最聪明的男孩终于首次通过了测试。

从那时起，史蒂夫就好像换了个人。虽然家庭生活依旧，但他的生活确实发生了变化。他发觉自己不仅能学习，而且能学得很好！他发现自己能理解并牢记所学知识，并能学以致用。史蒂夫开始变得优秀了，而且他在整个求学生涯中，一直都保持着优秀。

高中毕业后，史蒂夫应征加入了海军，他的军旅生涯也很成功。期间，他结识了他的爱人，组建了家庭，并从 Magna Cum Laude 大学毕业。他在海军服军役期间，曾鼓励过许多年轻人。假如没有他，这些人或许不可能建立自信，实现自身价值。从海军退役后，史蒂夫开始了他的第二份工作——在附近的一所大学担任助理教授，继续鼓舞他人。

怀特小姐留下了一份宝贵遗产，她挽救了一个男孩，这个男孩使许多生命发生了变化。我对这一切都很了解，因为我就是他的爱人。

你看，事情就这么简单。一个男孩的内心世界，只因一个老师的关心，就发生了如此大的变化。

爱和微笑，人生的芳醇

核心单词

remarkably [ri'mɑːkəb(ə)li] *adv.* 引人注目地；明显地；非常地

sharp [ʃɑːp] *adj.* 锋利的；尖的；陡的，机警的

entire [in'taiə] *adj.* 全部的，整个的

impatient [im'peiʃənt] *adj.* 无耐心的，不耐烦的；无法忍受的

hesitate ['heziteit] *v.* 踌躇；有疑虑，不愿意

severe [si'viə] *adj.* 严重的；剧烈的；严厉的；苛刻的

retain [ri'tein] *v.* 保留，保持

military ['militəri] *adj.* 军事的；军用的

legacy ['legəsi] *n.* 遗产；遗赠

实用句型

As he sat down，he couldn't resist another look at the lovely woman.

坐下之后，他情不自禁地又瞄了一眼这位漂亮的女子。

①As 在这里作连词，引导时间状语从句。

②look at 看，类似的表达还有 look over 仔细检查；look forward to 盼望；look into 研究，调查等固定搭配。

翻译行不行

1. 尽管遇到很多挫折，他仍坚持做实验。(in spite of)

....

2. 他的梦想是成为一名飞行员。(dream of)

....

3. 篮球赛何时举行？(take place)

....

Power in Gratitude
感恩的力量

· Meade ·

When my older son was **diagnosed** with Attention Deficit Hyperactivity Disorder, my first reaction was relief—I finally knew the reason for his behavior. However, I was also **overwhelmed** with sadness, fear and anger. I felt sorry for my son and for myself. Like many others in similar circumstances, my question to God was "Why me?"

Through the grace of God, I am now able to focus on my gratitude. I believe God chose me to raise my son because He knew that I would give him the best I have. He will teach me to love and understand him for who he is. I am grateful that I have my son, and grateful that God chose me to be his mother.

There is power and healing in gratitude.

How can gratitude help us in our everyday lives as moms? Think about the difference you can make in your family's life just by **noticing** and being thankful for all the great things they do. When you express gratitude, you show your love and appreciation. Everyone needs to feel these things every day. Sometimes as moms we feel that no one appreciates us—and it is true that moms are usually last on the list to be thanked. One way you can teach gratitude is by example. Even on the days when it seems your children or husband are doing everything wrong, find a reason to thank them. Take the time and energy to look for the good. Think about the things that your family does that deserve a "Thank you". You might say to your husband, "Thank you for working so hard for our family," or, to your child, "I really appreciate your sense of humor—it feels good to laugh." Expressing your gratitude helps family members to understand how it feels to be appreciated. And if they still don't catch on, let them know when you feel unappreciated. You can also tell them how great it makes you feel when they do express gratitude.

Gratitude is a wonderful motivator when you need cooperation. When enlisting the help of my two year old, I praise him often and with enthusiasm. I let him know that he is a great helper. I know I am teaching him appreciation because he expresses it to me. The other day I brought a bunch of multicolored roses home. For five days, at least once or twice a day, my son thanked me for the flowers.

Sometimes we get so busy and caught up in daily life that we forget to be grateful. We expect everyone to do their share without being asked. The only time anyone hears anything is when a chore has not been completed. This attitude, over the long haul, will develop very resentful and uncooperative family members.

When life is good, gratitude is easy. It becomes more challenging to be grateful when we are experiencing hard times.

Financial hardship, long-term illness, the death of a loved one and **marital** strife can all be trying and difficult. It is hard to find anything to be grateful for. But while pain is inevitable, suffering is optional. We have a choice in how we view our circumstances. We can turn our hearts to God and trust that he has a plan for us. We can be thankful for the lessons we learn and the opportunities for personal growth and transformation. Look at all the people in this world who share the gifts they received during especially difficult times of their life. It is the painful times of my life that have made me stronger, wiser, and more loving today.

I recently attended a powerful seminar on the various levels of energy that a human being **emanates**. The presenter identified seven different levels of energy. *The first level of energy is defined by feelings of apathy and thoughts of victimization*. A person at a level two energy has feelings of anger and thoughts of **conflict**. As a person moves up the energy scale, their feelings and thoughts are more positive. At level seven, one would experience unconditional love and no judgmental thoughts. Only God **radiates** at level seven. The average person emits energy at a level of 2. 5. To experience peace and joy,an individual must raise his energy level to 5 or 6.

So how can we raise our energy level and open our heart to joy? One powerful way is to develop an attitude of gratitude. Look at everyone with grateful eyes. Listen to your heart and the heart of your loved ones. Speak words of affirmation every day of your life. Be grateful for your life with all its lessons and blessings. The more grateful thoughts and feelings you experience and express the more **instrumental** you will be in healing the world. And your outlook on life will improve in the process.

米　德

　　当我的大儿子被确诊为"注意力缺陷多动症"时，我的第一反应就是放松——我终于知道他那些行为举止的原因所在了。然而，我也陷入了悲伤、畏惧和愤怒的深渊。我既为儿子也为我自己感到难过。像其他很多处于相似境况的人一样，我也禁不住要问上帝："为什么是我？"

　　由于上帝的恩惠，我现在可以把心思集中在感恩上了。我相信，上帝选择我来养育我的儿子，是因为他相信我会把我最好的东西给予儿子。上帝教导我去爱、去理解儿子的一切。我很感激上帝选择我做儿子的母亲。

　　感恩的力量和疗伤的作用是不可忽视的。

　　作为母亲，感恩在日常生活中又能如何帮助我们呢？通过注意和感谢家人所做的一切好的事情，想想你能为家庭生活带来什么变化。当你表示感恩的时候，你的爱心和感激也就表露无遗。每人每天都需要这些感受。作为母亲，有时候会感到没有人感激我们——事实也是如此，母亲总是最后一个被感谢的人。你传授感恩的一个方法就是自己树立榜样。即便有一天你的孩子和丈夫把所有的事情都搞错了，你也要找个理由感谢他们。你可以花些时间和精力，寻找他们做得好的地方。想想你的家人所做的事情，哪些值得你说一句"谢谢"。你可以对丈夫说一句："谢谢你为我们的家努力工作。"或者对孩子说，"我非常欣赏你的幽默感——笑一笑真好。"表达你的感激会帮助你的家人理解被他人感激的心情。如果他们还是无法领悟，那就在你需要感激的时候提醒他们。你也可以告诉他们，当他们向你表达感激时，带给你的美好感受。

在你需要合作的时候，感激之情就是一股巨大的推动力。当我获得我两岁儿子的帮助时，我经常满怀激情地表扬他。我要让他知道他帮了我很大的忙。我知道，因为他要感激我，所以我就要教他学会感激。几天前，我带回家一束颜色各异的玫瑰花，一连五天，他几乎每天都要说几次谢谢。

有时，我们过于繁忙，忙于芜杂的生活琐事，连感激都忘记了。我们期望每个人都能够自觉地尽职尽责。这种态度，日积月累，在家人之间就会发展为抱怨与不和。

生活安稳的时候，表达感激就会很简单。但是，当我们面对艰辛的生活时，表达感激就很难了。经济困难，长期疾病，亲人过世和婚姻纠纷都可能让人心烦，给生活带来困难。这时候，甚至连找一个感激的理由都很难。虽然痛苦无法避免，但我们有权选择是否接受痛苦，有权选择我们该如何看待我们周围的环境。我们可以相信上帝，相信上帝会给我们做好安排的。我们感激已有的经验教训，感激给个人成长和变化的机遇。看看大千世界中的芸芸众生，他们在生活的艰难中获得了礼物。正是生活中的那些痛苦时期让我更加坚强，更加聪明，更加热爱今天！

最近，我参加了一个很有影响的研讨班，讨论的主题是人类产生的多级能量。与会者把能量分成了七级。第一级能量是根据冷漠的感情和牺牲他人的思想而定义的；第二级能量的人怀有愤怒的感情和对抗的思想。人的能量级别越高，他的感情和思想也就越积极。在第 7 级别，人就会获得自由的爱和辩证的思想。只有上帝才能达到第 7 级。人类平均拥有的能量级别为 2．5 级。要想拥有和平和欢乐，个人的能量级别必须达到 5 级或 6 级。

那么我们该如何提高我们的能量级别呢？该如何敞开胸怀拥抱欢乐呢？一个有效的方法就是养成感激的态度。看看那些感激的眼神，聆听你的内心和你所爱的人的内心的声音，每天说些肯定的话，感激你生命中所拥有的教训和祝福。你拥有的感激的思想和感情越多，你对社会的作用就越大，你对生命的见解也就越深。

核心单词

diagnose ['daiəgnəuz] *v.* 诊断

overwhelm [,əuvə'hwelm] *v.* 战胜；征服；压倒

notice ['nəutis] *n.* 公告，通知，贴示

marital ['mæritl] *adj.* 婚姻的；夫妻的

emanate ['eməneit] *v.* (气体等) 发出，散发；放射

conflict ['kɔnflikt] *n.* 冲突，抵触，分歧 *v.* 矛盾，冲突

radiate ['reidieit] *v.* (光、热等) 散发，辐射；显出

instrumental [,instru'mentl] *adj.* 可作为手段的；有帮助的

实用句型

The first level of energy is defined by feelings of apathy and thoughts of victimization.

第一级能量是根据冷漠的感情和牺牲他人的思想而定义的。

①这是一个被动句，be defined by... 由（以）……而定义的。

②think of 想到，考虑，类似的表达还有 think about 考虑；think over 仔细考虑等固定搭配。

翻译行不行

1. 她正在寻找丢失的孩子。(look for)

....

2. 这首歌很好，我认为它会很快流行起来的。(catch on)

....

3. 你不管怎样该给个答复吧。(at least)

....

My Life Was Saved by a Smile
一个微笑挽救了一条生命

• Tracy Anderson •

I was sure that I was to be killed. I became **terribly** nervous. I fumbled in my pockets to see if there were any cigarettes, which had escaped their search. I found one and because of my shaking hands, I could barely get it to my lips. But I had no matches, they had taken those.

I looked through the bars at my jailer. He did not make eye contact with me. I called out to him, "Have you got a light?" He looked at me, shrugged and came over to light my cigarette.

"As he came close and lit the match, his eyes **inadvertently** locked with mine. At that moment, I smiled. I don't know why I did that. Perhaps it was nervousness, perhaps it was because, when you get very close, one to another, it is very hard not to smile. In any case, I smiled. In that instant, it was as though a spark jumped across the gap between our two hearts, our two human souls. I know he didn't want to, but my smile leaped through the bars and **generated** a smile on his lips, too.

He lit my cigarette but stayed near, looking at me directly in the eyes and continuing to smile. I kept smiling at him, now aware of him as a person and not just a jailer. And his looking at me seemed to have a new dimension too.

"Do you have kids?" he asked. "Yes, here, here." I took out my wallet and nervously **fumbled** for the pictures of my family. He, too, took out the pictures of his family and began to talk about his plans and hopes for them. My eyes filled with tears. *I said that I feared that I'd never see my family again, never have the chance to see them grow up.* Tears came to his eyes, too.

Suddenly, without another word, he unlocked my cell and silently led me out. Out of the jail, quietly and by back routes, out of the town. There, at the edge of town, he **released** me. And without another word, he turned back toward the town.

My life was saved by a smile. Yes, the smile—the unaffected, unplanned, natural connection between people. I really believe that if that part of you and that part of me could recognize each other, we wouldn't be enemies. We couldn't have hate or **envy** or fear.

特雷西·安德森

一想到自己明天就没命了，不禁陷入极端的惶恐之中。我翻遍了口袋，终于找到一支没被他们搜走的香烟，但我的手紧张地不停发抖，连将烟送进嘴里都成了问题，而我的火柴也在搜身时被拿走了。

我透过铁栏望着外面的警卫，他并没有注意到我在看他，我叫了他一声："能跟你借个火吗？"他转头望着我，耸了耸肩，然后走了过来，点燃我的香烟。

当他帮我点火时，他的眼光无意中扫过我的脸，这时我突然冲着他微笑。我不知道自己为何有这般反应，也许是过于紧张，或者是当你如此靠近一个人时，很难不对他微笑。不管是出于什么理由，我对他笑了。就在这一刹那，这抹微笑如同火花般，打破了我们心灵间的隔阂。受到了我的感染，他的嘴角也不自觉地现出了笑容，虽然我知道这并不是他的原意。

他点完火后并没立刻离开，两眼盯着我看，脸上仍带着微笑。我也以笑容回应，仿佛他是我的朋友，而不是守着我的警卫。他看着我的眼神也少了当初的那股凶气。

"你有小孩吗？"他开口问道。

"有，你看。"我拿出了皮夹，手忙脚乱地翻出了我的全家福照片。他也掏出了照片，并且开始讲述他对家人的期望与计划。这时我眼中充满了泪水，我说我害怕再也见不到家人。我害怕没机会看着孩子长大。他听着也流下了两行热泪。

突然间，他二话不说地打开了牢门，悄悄地带我从后面的小路逃离了监狱，出了小镇，就在小镇的边上，他放了我，之后便转身往回走，不曾留下一句话。

一个微笑居然能救自己一条命。是的，微笑是人与人之间最自然真挚的沟通方式。如果我们能用心灵去认识彼此，世间不会有结怨成仇的憾事；恨意、妒忌、恐惧也就不复存在了。

核心单词

terribly ['terəbli] *adv.* 可怕地；很，非常
inadvertently [ɪnəd'vɜ:təntli] *adv.* 不慎地；非故意地
generate ['dʒenə‚reit] *v.* 产生，发生；造成，引起
fumble ['fʌmbl] *v.* 乱摸；摸索
release [ri'li:s] *v.* 释放，解放；放松，松开
envy ['envi] *n.* 妒忌；羡慕

实用句型

I said that I feared that I'd never see my family again, never have the chance to see them grow up.

我说我害怕再也见不到家人。我害怕没机会看着孩子长大。

①这里的 I'd 是 I would 的省略形式。

②see 后用不带 to 的不定式，类似的词还有 help；suggest；hope 等。

翻译行不行

1. 他们从南方远道来看我。（come over）

....

2. 医生已拨掉了我的坏牙。（take out）

....

3. 积雪的山上挤满了年轻的滑雪者。（fill with）

....

The Price of a Miracle
奇迹的价格

• Jennifer Roberts •

Tess was eight years old when she heard her Mom and Dad talking about her little brother, Andrew. All she knew was that he was very sick and they were **completely** out of money. They were moving to an apartment complex next month because Daddy didn't have the money for both the doctor bills and the house payment.

Only a very **costly** surgery could save her brother now and it was looking like there was no one to loan them the money. She heard her Dad say to her Mom, "Only a miracle can save him now."

Tess went to her bedroom and pulled a glass jelly jar from its hiding place in the closet. She **poured** all the change out on the floor and counted it carefully. She counted it three times. The total had to be exactly perfect. No chance here for mistakes.

Carefully placing the coins back in the jar and twisting on the cap, she slipped out from the back door and made her way 6 blocks to Rexall's Drug Store with the big red Indian Chief sign above the door.

Tess waited patiently for the pharmacist to give her some attention but he was too intently talking to another man to be **bothered** by an eight year old at this moment. She twisted her feet to make a scuffing noise.

Nothing.

She cleared her throat with the most disgusting sound she could muster. No good.

Finally she took a **quarter** from her jar and banged it on the glass counter. That did it!

"And what do you want?" the pharmacist asked in an annoyed tone of voice. "I'm talking to my brother from Chicago whom I haven't seen in ages." he said without waiting for a reply to his question.

"Well, I want to talk to you about my brother." Tess answered back in the same annoyed tone, "He's really, really sick, and I want to buy a miracle."

"I beg your pardon?" said the pharmacist.

"His name is Andrew and he has something bad growing inside his head and my Daddy says only a miracle can save him now. So, how much does a miracle cost?"

"We don't sell miracles here, little girl. I'm sorry but I can't help you." the pharmacist said, softening a little.

"Listen, I have the money to pay for it. If it isn't enough, I will get the rest. Just tell me how much it costs."

The pharmacist's brother **stooped** down and asked the little girl, "What kind of a miracle does your brother need?"

"I don't know." Tess replied with her eyes welling up,

"I just know he's really sick and Mommy says he needs an operation, but my Daddy can't pay for it, so I want to use my money."

"How much do you have?" asked the pharmacist's brother.

"One dollar and eleven cents." Tess answered **barely** audiblely, "And it's all the money I have, but I can get some more if I need to."

"Well, what a coincidence." smiled the man. "A dollar and eleven cents... the exact price of a miracle for little brother." Then he said, "Take me to where you live. I want to see your brother and meet your parents. Let's see if I have the kind of miracle you need."

The pharmacist's brother was Dr. Carlton Armstrong, a surgeon from Chicago who specialized in neuro-surgery. The operation was completed without charge and it wasn't long until Andrew was home again and doing well. Later, Mom and Dad were talking about the chain of events that had led them to this. Her mom said, "That surgery was a real miracle. I wonder how much it would have cost?" Tess smiled. She knew exactly how much a miracle cost...One dollar and eleven cents. . . plus the **faith** of a little child.

詹妮弗·罗伯茨

8 岁的苔丝听爸爸妈妈谈论小弟弟安德鲁的事。她只知道弟弟病得很重，他们家钱都花光了。下个月他们就要搬到合住的公寓去了，因为爸爸已经没钱付弟弟的医疗费和房租了。

救治弟弟需要很昂贵的手术费用，而且也没人会借给他们钱。她听爸爸跟妈妈说："现在只有奇迹能救他了。"

苔丝走进了自己房间，从壁橱里隐秘的地方找出一个装果冻的玻璃罐子。她把里面所有的零钱都倒在地板上，仔细地数了起来，一共数了三遍，数目必须得准确，这就不会有错了。

她小心翼翼地把硬币装回罐子，拧上盖子，然后悄悄从后门溜了出去，走了六个街区来到"雷克索"药店，这家药店的大门上挂着大大的印第安酋长的标志。

苔丝耐心地等着药剂师能接待她，可那时药剂师正忙着与另一个人说话，根本顾不卜理这个 8 岁的孩子。她在地板上蹭着脚，摩擦出声。

没用。

她用她能发出的最让人恶心的声音清嗓子。还是没用。

最后她从罐子里拿出一个 25 分的硬币，"当"的扔在玻璃柜台上。这回管用了！

"你想要什么？"药剂师不耐烦地说："我正在和我的弟弟说话，他从芝加哥来，我们好多年没见了。"他不等回答就接着说。

"我想跟你说说我的弟弟。"苔丝也同样不耐烦地答道，"他病得很重很重，我想买一个'奇迹'。"

"你再说一遍？"药剂师说。

"他叫安德鲁，他脑袋里长了个坏东西，我爸爸说现在只有

Love and smile, the sweetest wine of life

爱和微笑，人生的芳醇

037

奇迹能救他。那么，'奇迹'要多少钱？"

"我们这不卖'奇迹'，小姑娘。对不起，我帮不了你。"药剂师说，语气柔和了许多。

"听我说，我有钱买。如果这个不够，我会再给，你就告诉我要多少钱吧。"

药剂师的弟弟俯下身，问苔丝："你弟弟需要什么样的奇迹？"

"我不知道，"苔丝的泪水夺眶而出，回答说，"我只知道他病得非常厉害，妈妈说他需要手术，但是爸爸付不起手术费，所以我想用我的钱。"

"你有多少钱？"药剂师的弟弟问。

"一块一毛一，"苔丝回答的声音别人几乎听不到，"这是我所有的钱，但是如果需要，我还可以再弄点来。"

"真是巧啊，"那人笑了。"一块一毛一……正好是治你弟弟的'奇迹'的价钱。"然后他说，"带我去你家，我想看看你弟弟，见见你父母。咱们看看我有没有你所说的'奇迹'。"

这个药剂师的弟弟是卡尔顿·阿姆斯特朗医生，芝加哥神经外科手术的专家。手术没要一分钱，没过多久，安德鲁就回家了，而且恢复得很好。后来，爸爸妈妈又谈起这件事的来龙去脉，妈妈说："这个手术真是一个奇迹，它到底需要多少钱呢？"苔丝笑了，她知道这个奇迹的确切价格是……一块一毛一，再加上一个孩子的信念。

Practising
& Exercise

实战
提升篇

核心单词

completely [kəm'pli:tli] *adv.* 完整地；完全地；彻底地

costly ['kɔstli] *adj.* 贵重的，宝贵的

pour [pɔ:] *v.* 倒，灌，注

bother ['bɔðə] *v.* 烦扰，打搅

quarter ['kwɔ:tə] *n.* 四分之一；一刻钟

stoop [stu:p] *v.* 屈身，弯腰

barely ['bɛəli] *adv.* 仅仅，勉强；几乎没有

faith [feiθ] *n.* 信念；信任，完全信赖

实用句型

The pharmacist's brother was Dr. Carlton Armstrong，a surgeon from Chicago who specialized in neuro-surgery.

药剂师的弟弟是卡尔顿·阿姆斯特朗医生，芝加哥神经外科手术的专家。

①这里是由 who 引导的定语从句。

②from 来自，也可说 come from。

翻译行不行

1. 我 8 点在这里等你。(wait for)

......

2. 那点轻微的损坏并减低不了引擎的威力。(take from)

......

3. 他昨晚 12 点才回到家。(not until)

......

The Roses from Heaven
来自天堂的玫瑰

• Henry Beecher •

Red roses were her favorites, her name was also Rose. And every year her husband sent them, tied with pretty bows. The year he died, the roses were **delivered** to her door. The card said, "Be my Valentine", like all the years before. Each year he sent her roses, and the note would always say, "I love you even more this year than last year on this day." "My love for you will always grow, with every passing year." She knew this was the last time that the roses would appear. She thought, he ordered roses in advance before this day. *Her loving husband did not know that he would pass away*. He always liked to do things early, way before the time. Then, if he got too busy, everything would work out fine.

She **trimmed** the stems, and placed them in a very special vase. Then, sat the vase beside the portrait of his smiling face, she would sit for hours in her husband's favorite chair, while staring at his picture, and the roses sitting there. A year went by, and it was hard to live without her mate, with loneliness and solitude, that had become her fate. Then, the very hour, as on Valentines before, the doorbell rang, and there were roses, sitting by her door. She brought the roses in, and then just looked at them in shock. Then, went to get the telephone to call the florist shop, the owner answered and she asked him if he would explain, why would someone do this to her, **causing** her such pain? "I know your husband passed away, more than a year ago," The owner said, "I knew you'd call and you would want to know. The flowers you received today were paid for in advance. Your husband always planned ahead, he left nothing to change. There is a standing order that I have on file down here, and he has paid, well in advance, you'll get them every year. There also is another thing that I think you should know. He wrote a special little card. . . he did it years ago. Then, should ever I find out that he's no longer here, that's the card. . . that should be sent to you the following year." She thanked him and hung up the phone, her tears now flowing hard. Her fingers shaking as she slowly reached to get the card. Inside the card, she saw that he had written her a note. Then, as she stared in total **silence**, this is what he wrote... "Hello, my love, I know it's been a year since I've been gone, I hope it hasn't been too hard for you to overcome. I know it must be lonely, and the pain is very real. For if it were the other way, I know how I would feel. The love we shared made everything so beautiful in life. I loved you more than words can say, you were the perfect wife. You were my friend and lover, you **fulfilled** my every need. I know it's only been a year, but please try not to grieve. I want you to be happy, even when you shed your tears. That is why the roses will be sent to you for years. When you get these roses, think of all the happiness that we had together and how both of us were blessed. I have always loved you and I know I always will. But, my love, you must go on, you have some living still. Please... try to find happiness, while living out your days. I know it is not easy, but I hope you find some ways. The roses will come every year and they will only stop when your door is not answered when the **florist** stops to knock. He will come five times that day, in case you have gone out. But after his last visit, he will know without a doubt to take the roses to the place where I've **instructed** him. And place the roses where we are, together once again."

亨利·比彻

　　罗丝最喜欢红玫瑰，她的名字也是玫瑰的意思。每年，丈夫都会送给她一些玫瑰花，花上系着漂亮的丝带。这一年，她丈夫去世了，玫瑰花却依然送到了她的门前，卡片上写着和往年一样的话语：做我的妻子吧！年年送花,他都写这样的话："对你的爱今朝更胜往年，时光流转爱你越来越多。"她想，今年的玫瑰一定是丈夫提前预定的。以后再也不会有玫瑰花了。她心爱的丈夫并不知道自己会逝去。他总是喜欢把事情提前安排妥当，以往即使再忙，凡事都能从容办好。

　　罗丝修整了花束，把玫瑰插进一只很特别的花瓶里，花瓶旁摆放着丈夫满面笑容的遗像。她在丈夫心爱的椅子里一坐就是几个小时，伴着玫瑰花，痴望着他的相片，沉浸在美好的回忆中。一年过去了，失去了丈夫的日子十分难熬，孤独和寂寞占据了她的生命。情人节前夕，门铃响了，有人送来了玫瑰花。她把花拿进来，非常惊讶。于是她打电话给花店，"是谁在恶作剧，为什么要惹我伤心？"店主解释说："我知道您的丈夫一年前去世了，也知道您会打电话来询问究竟。您今天收到的花，是您丈夫提前预订的。您丈夫总是提前做好计划，万无一失。他预付了货款，委托我们每年送花给您。还有一件事我想您应该知道，就在去年他还写了一张特别的小卡片，嘱咐着：如果他不在了，卡片就在第二年送给您。"她谢过店主，挂上了电话，顿时泪如泉涌，手指颤抖着慢慢地打开了附在玫瑰花上的卡片。卡片里是一张写给她的便条。她静静地看着："你好吗，我的妻子？我知道我已经去世一年了，我希望挺过这一年的你没有受太多的苦。我知道你一定很孤单，很痛苦。我们的爱使生活里的一切如此美好，任何语言都表达不了我对你的爱，你是完美的妻子，是我的朋友和情人，让我心满意足。时光只过去了一年，请不要悲伤，我要你即使流泪也是幸福的，这就是为什么年年都会送你玫瑰花的原因。当你收到玫瑰的时候，想想我们在一起时的快乐吧，我们曾经是多么幸福。我很爱你，我也会永远地爱你。但是，我的妻子，你一定要好好地活着啊！请……珍惜生命，追寻幸福吧。我知道那不容易，但是你一定要想想办法。玫瑰花每年都会如期而至，除非你不再应门，花店才会停止送花。那一天，花店的伙计会上门来访五次，以防你偶尔出门去了。但是，访问过五次之后，他就可以确认：这些花该送到我指示给他的另一个地方——我们重逢相聚的地方。"

核心单词

deliver [di'livə] *v.* 投递；传送；运送

trim [trim] *v.* 修剪；整理

cause [kɔ:z] *n.* 原因；起因

silence ['sailəns] *n.* 无声；沉默，默不作声

fulfill [ful'fil] *v.* 执行（命令等）；服从；履行（诺言等）

bless [bles] *v.* 为……祝福，为……祈神赐福；保佑

florist ['flɔrist] *n.* 花商，种花者

instruct [in'strʌkt] *v.* 指示，命令，吩咐

实用句型

Her loving husband did not know that he would pass away.

她心爱的丈夫并不知道自己会逝去。

①这里是由 that 引导的宾语从句。

② pass away 去世，类似的表达还有 pass by 经过；pass off 消失等固定搭配。

翻译行不行

1. 仪仗队走在前面。(in advance)

....

2. 我不再是个学生了。(no longer)

....

3. 如果她回来了，请立刻告诉我。(in case)

....

Forever Sisters
永远的两姐妹

· Donald ·

Today we are reading a story about two sisters. Their names were Sandy and Candy. They were very lonely. When their mother died, Sandy was only a **junior** high student, and Candy was an **elementary** school student. Their father was a gambler. He gambled nights and days and finally ended up in high debt. So, to avoid repaying the money, he ran away and left the two sisters behind.

At that time their mother had been dead for five years. After their father walked out on them, the two sisters could only stay at a friend's house, because their own house was given away to repay their father's debt. But the two sisters never **feared** hardship and did not lose hope for a better life. They lived their lives happily and actively.

The two sisters were both very hardworking. After school, Sandy, the elder sister, did everything she could to **support** the family. She sold newspapers and sometimes worked as a tutor to earn **extra** money. And Candy, the younger sister, prepared meals and did all the chores at home. Though the younger sister was small, she could manage money very well. The two sisters cared for each other. And their school grades were excellent.

Now, the two sisters are still in poverty. *But their stories have touched a lot of people*, *and they help the two sisters in anyway they can.* The landlord, the bathhouse keeper, the shop owners, their schoolmates and teachers in the same neighborhood are all looking after them. Poor as they are, they say they are the happiest persons in the world because they can be with each other every day.

唐纳德

今天我们来读一个关于两姊妹的故事。两姊妹的名字叫珊蒂与坎蒂。她们非常寂寞。当她们的母亲去世时，珊蒂还只个是中学生，而坎蒂只是一个小学生。她们的父亲是一个赌徒，从早到晚只知道赌博，最后落得债台高筑，为了逃避赌债，他丢下两姊妹跑掉了。

那时母亲也已经去世五年了。父亲遗弃她们后，两姐妹只能住在朋友家，因为她们自家的房子已经拿去抵债了。但两姐妹不害怕艰辛，仍然对未来抱持着美好的希望，开朗快乐地过着每一天。

两姊妹都非常勤奋。珊蒂利用课余时间打工赚钱养家。她送报纸，有时做家教赚钱。妹妹坎蒂在家负责做饭、打扫等一切家事，她年纪虽小，却能掌管好金钱。两姐妹互相关心，两人在学校的成绩都很突出。

如今，她们依然贫困。但她们的故事感动了许多人，大家纷纷从各方面帮助她们。住在同一社区的房东、管澡堂的婆婆、商店老板，以及她们的同学和老师，都照顾着她们。虽然生活贫困艰辛，但对她们两人来说，每天都能在一起就是最大的幸福。

Practising
& Exercise

实战
提升篇

核心单词

junior ['dʒuːnjə] *adj.* 资浅的；晚辈的

elementary [ˌeliˈmentəri] *adj.* 基本的；初级的

fear [fiə] *n.* 害怕，恐惧

support [səˈpɔːt] *v.* 支撑，支托，扶持

extra ['ekstrə] *adj.* 额外的；外加的

实用句型

But their stories have touched a lot of people，and they help the two sisters in anyway they can.

但她们的故事感动了许多人，大家纷纷从各方面帮助她们。

① in anyway they can 是省略了 that 的方式状语从句。

② a lot of 许多，类似的表达还有 lots of 许多的等。

翻译行不行

1. 你要是老这样花钱，总有一天要负债的。（end up）

....

2. 在婚礼上，新娘由其父亲交给新郎。（give away）

....

3. 你上班时谁来照料你的孩子？（look after）

....

That's What Friends Do
朋友间就该这么做

· Elliott ·

Jack tossed the papers on my desk— his eyebrows' knit into a straight line as he glared at me.

"What's wrong?" I asked.

He jabbed a finger at the **proposal**. "Next time you want to change anything, ask me first," he said, turning on his heels and leaving me stewing in anger.

How dare he treat me like that, I thought. I had changed one long sentence, and corrected grammar— something I thought I was paid to do.

It's not that I hadn't been warned. The other women, who had served in my place before me, called him names I couldn't repeat. One co-worker took me aside the first day. "He's personally responsible for two different secretaries leaving the firm," she whispered.

As the weeks went by, I grew to **despise** Jack. It was against everything I believed in— turn the other cheek and love your enemies. But Jack quickly slapped a verbal insult on any cheek turned his way. I prayed about it, but to be honest, I wanted to put him in his place, not love him.

One day, another of his episodes left me in tears. I stormed into his office, prepared to lose my job if needed, but not before I let the man know how I felt. I opened the door and Jack glanced up.

"What?" he said abruptly.

Suddenly I knew what I had to do. After all, he deserved it.

I sat across from him. "Jack, the way you've been treating me is wrong. I've never had anyone speak to me that way. As a **professional**, it's wrong, and it's wrong for me to allow it to continue." I said.

Jack snickered nervously and leaned back in his chair. I closed my eyes briefly. God help me, I prayed.

"I want to make you a promise. I will be a friend," I said, "I will treat you as you deserve to be treated, with respect and kindness. You deserve that," I said, "Everybody does." I slipped out of the chair and closed the door behind me.

Jack avoided me the rest of the week. Proposals, specs, and letters appeared on my desk while I was at lunch, and the **corrected** versions were not seen again. I brought cookies to the office one day and left a batch on Jack's desk. Another day I left a note. "Hope your day is going great," it read.

Over the next few weeks, Jack reappeared. He was reserved, but there were no other episodes. Co-workers cornered me in the break room.

"Guess you got to Jack," they said, "you must have told him off good." I shook my head. "Jack and I are becoming friends," I said in faith. I refused to talk about him. Every time

I saw Jack in the hall, I smiled at him. After all, that's what friends do.

One year after our "talk", I discovered I had breast cancer. I was 32, the mother of three beautiful young children, and scared. The cancer had metastasized to my lymph nodes and the **statistics** were not great for long-term survival. After surgery, I visited friends and loved ones who tried to find the right words to say. No one knew what to say. Many said the wrong things. Others wept, and I tried to **encourage** them. I clung to hope.

The last day of my hospital stay, the door darkened and Jack stood awkwardly on the threshold. I waved him in with a smile and he walked over to my bed and, without a word, placed a bundle beside me. Inside lay several bulbs.

"Tulips," he said.

I smiled, not understanding.

He cleared his throat. "If you plant them when you get home, they'll come up next spring." He shuffled his feet. "I just wanted you to know that I think you'll be there to see them when they come up."

Tears clouded my eyes and I reached out my hand.

"Thank you," I whispered.

Jack grasped my hand and gruffly replied, "You're welcome. You can't see it now, but next spring you'll see the colors I picked out for you." He turned and left without a word.

I have seen those red and white striped tulips push through the soil every spring for over ten years now. In fact, this September the doctor will declare me cured. I've seen my

爱和微笑，人生的芳醇

051

children graduate from high school and enter college.

In a moment when I prayed for just the right word，a man with very few words said all the right things.

After all，that's what friends do.

艾略特

杰克把文件扔到我桌上，皱着眉头，气愤地瞪着我。

"怎么了？"我问道。

他狠狠地指着计划书说："下次做什么改动前，先征求一下我的意见。"然后转身走了，留下我一个人在那里生闷气。

他怎能这样对我！我想，我只是改了一个长句，更正了语法错误，但这都是我的分内之事。

其实也有人提醒过我，我的上一任就曾大骂过他。我第一天上班时，就有同事把我拉到一旁小声说："他已经辞掉两个秘书了。"

几周后，我逐渐对杰克有些鄙视了，而这又有悖于我的信条——有人打你的左脸，你要把右脸也伸过去，要爱自己的敌人。但无论怎么做，总会挨杰克的骂。说真的，我很想灭灭他嚣张的气焰，而不是去爱他。我还为此默默祈祷过。

一天，因为一件事，我又被他气哭了。我冲进他的办公室，准备在被炒鱿鱼前让他知道我的感受。我推开门，杰克抬头看了我一眼。

"有事吗？"他突然说道。

我猛地意识到该怎么做了。毕竟，他罪有应得。

我在他对面坐下，"杰克，你对待我的方式有很大的问题。没人对我说过那样的话。作为一个职业人士，你这么做是不对的，我不该容忍这样的事情持续存在。"

杰克不安地笑了笑，向后靠了靠。我闭了一下眼睛，祈祷着，希望上帝能帮帮我。

"我保证自己可以成为你的朋友。我会尊敬你，礼貌地对待你，这是我应做的。每个人都应得到这样的礼遇。"我说完后，就起身离开了。

那个星期余下的几天，杰克一直躲着我。他总趁我吃午饭时，把计划书、技术说明和信件放在我桌上，并且，我修改过的文件不再被打回了。一天，我买了些饼干去办公室，顺便在杰克桌上留了一包。第二天，我又留了一张字条，写道："祝你今天一切顺利。"

接下来的几个星期，杰克不再躲避我了，但沉默了许多，办公室里也没再发生不愉快的事情。于是，同事们在休息室把我团团围了起来。

"听说杰克被你镇住了，"他们说，"你肯定大骂了他一顿。"我摇了摇头，一字一顿地说："我们会成为朋友。"我没有和人们说太多别的话。每次在大厅看见他时，我总冲他微笑。毕竟，朋友就该这样。

一年后，我32岁，是3个漂亮孩子的母亲。但我被确诊为乳腺癌，这让我极端恐惧。癌细胞已经扩散到我的淋巴腺。根据临床数值来看，我时日不多了。手术后，我拜访了亲朋好友，他们都尽力宽慰我，可不知道说什么好，有些人反而说错话了，

爱和微笑，人生的芳醇

另外一些人则为我难过，还得我去安慰他们。我始终没有放弃希望。

就在我出院的前一天，门外有个人影，是杰克，他尴尬地站在门口。我微笑着招呼他进来，他走到我床边，默默地把一包东西放在我旁边，那里边是几个球茎。

"这是郁金香。"他说。

我笑着，不明白他的用意。

他清了清嗓子，"回家后把它们种下，到明年春天就长出来了。"他挪了挪脚，"我希望你知道，你一定看得到它们发芽开花。"

我泪眼朦胧地伸出手。

"谢谢你。"我低声说。

杰克抓住我的手，生硬地说："不必客气。到明年长出来后，你就能看到我为你挑的是什么颜色的郁金香了。"而后，他没说一句话便转身离开了。

转眼间，十多年过去了，每年春天，我都会看着这些红白相间的郁金香破土而出。事实上，到今年九月，医生就会宣布我已痊愈了。我的孩子们也都高中毕业，进入了大学。

在那绝望的时刻，我祈求他人的安慰，而这个男人仅用寥寥数语，却情真意切，温暖着我脆弱的心。

毕竟，朋友之间就该这么做。

Practising

& Exercise

核心单词

propose [prə'pəuz] v. 提议，建议，提出

despise [dis'paiz] v. 鄙视；看不起

professional [prə'feʃənl] adj. 职业（上）的；从事特定专业

correct [kə'rekt] adj. 正确的，对的

statistics [stə'tistiks] n. 统计，统计资料

encourage [in'kʌridʒ] v. 鼓励；怂恿

实用句型

It's not that I hadn't been warned. 其实已经有人提醒过我了。

①双重否定表肯定。

② warn 警告，告诫，另外有 warn off 警告……不得靠近；warn against 告诫……当心等搭配。

翻译行不行

1. 你不要根据外表来判断。（go by）

....

2. 猴子从栏杆里伸出手拿走了香蕉。（reach out）

....

3. 我来替你挑几个吧。（pick out）

....

A Church Built with 57 Cents
57 美分建成的教堂

• Anonymous •

A sobbing little girl stood near a small church from which she had been turned away because it was too crowded. "I can't go to Sunday School." she sobbed to the **pastor** as he walked by. Seeing her shabby, unkempt appearance, the pastor guessed the reason and, taking her by the hand, took her inside and found a place for her in the Sunday School class. The child was so **touched** that she went to bed that night thinking of the children who have no place to worship Jesus.

Some two years later, this child lay dead in one of the poor **tenement** buildings and the parents called for the kindhearted pastor, who had befriended their daughter, to handle the final arrangements. As her poor little body was being moved, a worn and **crumpled** purse was found which seemed to have been rummaged from some trash dump. Inside was found 57 cents and a note scribbled in childish handwriting which read, "This is to help build the little church bigger so more children can go to Sunday school."

For two years she had saved for this offering of love. When

the pastor tearfully read that note, he knew **instantly** what he would do.

Carrying this note and the cracked, red pocketbook to the pulpit, he told the story of her unselfish love and devotion. He challenged his deacons to get busy and raise enough money for the larger building.

But the story does not end there!

A newspaper learned of the story and **published** it. *It was read by a realtor who offered them a parcel of land worth many thousands*. When told that the church could not pay so much, he offered it for a 57 cent payment.

Church members made large **subscriptions**. Checks came from far and wide. Within five years the little girl's gift had increased to $250, 000, 00, a huge sum at that time (near the turn of the century). Her unselfish love had paid large dividends.

When you are in the city of Philadelphia, look up Temple Baptist Church, with a seating **capacity** of 3, 300, and Temple University, where hundreds of students are trained. Have a look, too, at the Good Samaritan Hospital and at a Sunday School building which houses hundreds of Sunday scholars, so that no child in the area will ever need to be left outside at Sunday school time.

In one of the rooms of this building may be seen the picture of the sweet face of the little girl whose 57 cents, so sacrificially saved, made such **remarkable** history. Alongside of it is a portrait of her kind pastor, Dr. Russell H. Conwell, author of the book, *Acres of Diamonds*, a true story.

佚　名

　　小女孩站在一座小教堂旁边哭泣，因为"太拥挤"，教堂不让她进。"我去不成主日学校了。"她抽搭着，对走过的牧师说道。看着她褴褛的衣着，蓬乱的头发，牧师猜到了原因，便牵起她的手，将她带进教堂并在主日学校里给她找到了座位。小女孩非常感动，那夜入睡的时候她还在想着那些没有地方做礼拜的孩子们。

　　大概两年后，孩子在一个破旧的棚户区死去了。她的父母请来了好心的牧师——他已经和小女孩成了朋友，请他为小女孩主持葬礼。当她小小的身体被搬起的时候，一个破旧而且皱巴巴的钱包掉了出来，那看上去像是从垃圾堆里拣来的。里面有 57 美分，还有一张字条，上面用童稚的字体歪歪扭扭地写着："这是扩建小教堂的钱，好让更多的孩子能去主日学校。"

　　她为了这份爱的礼物攒了两年。当牧师眼含泪水地读着这张纸条的时候，他忽然醒悟到自己该做什么了。

　　他带着这张纸条和那个破旧的红色钱包去到讲坛，向大家讲述了这个小女孩的故事，以及她的无私和虔诚。他要求教堂执事发起募捐来扩建教堂。

　　不过，故事到这里并没有完。

　　一家报纸报道了这个故事。一个房地产商人读了以后提供了一块价值好几千块的土地。当得知教堂付不起时，他开出的价格是 57 美分。

教堂成员捐出了很多钱。支票从很远的地方源源不断寄来。5 年间，小女孩的礼物已经增加到了 25 万美元，在当时（十九世纪末）是一大笔钱。她无私的爱产生了高额的利息。

今天当你身处费城，该去看看那个高大的可容纳 3,300 人的坦普浸信会教堂，和能够容纳几百个学生的坦普大学。再看看那家好撒玛利亚人医院，和容纳几百人的主日学校。再也不会有孩子被阻隔在主日学校门外了。

在这个主日学校的一个房间里，你会看见那个有着甜美笑容的小女孩的照片，她那 57 美分的奉献已经创造了一段历史性的传奇。在她照片的旁边是那个善良的牧师的照片，著名的罗素·康威尔博士。他就是《钻石宝地》的作者。这是一个真实的故事。

核心单词

pastor ['pɑːstə] *n.* （基督教的）本堂牧师

touch [tʌtʃ] *v.* 接触，碰到

tenement ['tenimənt] *n.* 廉价公寓

crumple ['krʌmpl] *v.* 弄皱，压皱

instantly ['instəntli] *adv.* 立即，马上

publish ['pʌbliʃ] *v.* 出版；发行

subscription [sʌb'skripʃən] *n.* 捐款，认捐

capacity [kə'pæsiti] *n.* 容量，容积；能量

remarkable [ri'mɑːkəbl] *adj.* 非凡的；卓越的

实用句型

It was read by a realtor who offered them a parcel of land worth many thousands.

一个房地产商人读了以后提供了一块价值好几千块的土地。

①这里是由 who 引导的定语从句。

② a parcel of 一块，类似的表达还有 a piece of 一张，一片；a bunch of 一束，一串等固定搭配。

翻译行不行

1. 医生是不会见死不救的。（turn away）

....

2. 这是个迫切需要解决的问题。（call for）

....

3. 如果你有不认识的字就查查字典。（look up）

....

Love Needs No Words
大爱无声

· Unda Sledge ·

"Can I see my baby?" the happy new mother asked. When the **bundle** was nestled in her arms and she moved the fold of cloth to look upon his tiny face, she gasped. The doctor turned quickly and looked out the tall hospital window.

The baby had been born without ears. Time **proved** that the baby's hearing was perfect. It was only his appearance that was marred.

When he rushed home from school one day and flung himself into his mother's arms, she sighed, knowing that his life was to be a succession of heartbreaks. He blurted out the tragedy, "A boy, a big boy... called me a freak."

He grew up, handsome but for his misfortune. A **favorite** with his fellow students, he might have been class president, but for that. He developed a gift, a talent for literature and music.

The boy's father had a session with the family physician, "Could nothing be done?"

"I believe I could graft on a pair of outer ears, if they could be gotten." the doctor declared. *They searched for a person who would make such a great sacrifice for the young man.*

Two years went by. One day, his father said to the son, "You're going to the hospital, son. Mother and I have someone who will **donate** the ears you need. But the identity of the donor is a secret."

The operation was a brilliant success, and a new person emerged. His talents blossomed into genius. School and college became a series of triumphs. He married and enter the **diplomatic** service.

He would ask his father: "Who gave me the ears? Who gave me so much? I could never do enough for him or her."

"I do not believe you could," said the father, "but the agreement was that you are not to know... not yet."

The years kept their profound secret, but the day did come. He stood with his father over his mother's casket. Slowly, **tenderly**, the father stretched forth his hand and raised the thick, reddish-brown hair to reveal that the mother had no outer ears.

"Mother said she was glad she never got her hair cut," his father whispered gently, "and nobody ever thought mother less beautiful, did they?"

芸达·斯莱奇

"我能看看我的孩子吗？"刚刚做了母亲的女人高兴地问。当襁褓被放到她怀里，她拿开挡着孩子小脸的布时，她倒吸了一口凉气。医生快速地转过身去，向外望去。

孩子天生没有耳朵。事实证明他的听力完全没有问题。只是容貌上有缺陷。

一天,他从学校飞奔回家,投入妈妈的怀抱。她叹息着,知道他的一生将有一连串的伤心。他说出了那件让人心碎的事情:"一个男孩,大个子男孩,叫我怪物。"

他长大了,尽管有那个悲惨命运,他还是长得很英俊。他人缘很好,如果不是因为那个残疾,他本可以做班长的,他在文学和音乐方面很有天赋。

男孩的爸爸去问家庭医生:"难道真的一点办法也没有吗?"

"办法是有的。如果能找到一双合适的外耳,我可以帮他植入。"医生说。他们开始寻找看有谁愿意为年轻人做出这样的牺牲。

两年过去了。一天,父亲告诉儿子:"孩子,你终于可以做手术了。妈妈和我找到愿意为你捐耳朵的人了。但是,捐献者要求身份保密。"

手术非常成功,他脱胎换骨。他的才华宛如鲜花怒放般得到了释放。学业也取得了一连串的成功。后来,他结了婚,并做了外交官。

他问父亲:"是谁给了我耳朵?是谁如此地慷慨?我永远报答不尽。"

"我不认为你有那个能力去报答,"爸爸说,"我们当初协议中规定你不能知道是谁,至少现在还不能。"

父亲的守口如瓶使这个秘密保持了许多年,但是,这一天终于还是来了。他和爸爸站在妈妈的棺木前。慢慢地,轻柔地,爸爸伸出手撩起了妈妈那浓密的棕红色的头发,显露在孩子面前的竟是:妈妈没有耳朵!

"妈妈说她很庆幸自己从来不用去理发,"爸爸低声说道,"但没人会认为你母亲因此而减少了一丝一毫的美丽,不是吗?"

核心单词

bundle ['bʌndl] *n.* 捆，卷；包裹

prove [pruːv] *v.* 证明，证实

favorite ['feivərit] *n.* 特别喜爱的人（或物）；受宠的人

donate [dəu'neit] *v.* 捐献，捐赠

diplomatic [ˌdiplə'mætik] *adj.* 外交的；外交人员的

tenderly ['tendəli] *adv.* 温和地，柔和地，体贴地

实用句型

They searched for a person who would make such a great sacrifice for the young man .

他们开始找寻看有谁愿意为年轻人做出这样的牺牲。

① who 在这里修饰 a person。

② search for 搜查，搜寻，类似的表达还有 search into 探究，调查；search out 找到等固定搭配。

翻译行不行

1. 他一不留心说出了一个深藏心底的秘密。(blurt out)

....

2. 他今天穿了一双新鞋子。(a pair of)

....

3. 当心！你要撞到树了。(look out)

....

Kobe Bryant's Growing Road
小乔丹科比·布莱恩特的成长之路

Kobe Bryant first started turning heads on the basketball court when he was in middle school. His talents **dominated** the game so much that high shools from all over the Philadelphia area watched him grow up. The almost six-foot tall seventh grader definitely had the make-up and **genes** for the game, as his dad was former NBA forward, Joe Bryant. Kobe developed his basketball skills under the watchful eye of his father, helping his **mission** to become a professional basketball player. He worked daily on his game, watching video, playing in the playgrounds and listening to his father's advice.

When he entered high school in Philadelphia, Kobe was a highly touted **recruit**. He proved that he had the skills and work ethic to be a star at the next level and the **scouts** noticed this. Kobe didn't let anybody down either, as he played on the varsity basketball team his freshman year. He wouldn't immediately be a superstar, though. Rather it was the countless hours of early morning workouts by himself in the gymnasium that **escalated** Kobe's talents.

Kobe became a better player when he played in high school and soon enough, he had developed into one of the premier talents at the high school level. *He sold out the games everywhere he played during his junior and senior years and he didn't disappoint anyone*. He once packed the school gym so much that it caused a traffic jam on the main highway just outside the school.

He went on to finish his high school career as the all-time leading point scorer in Pennsylvania history with a total of 2,883 points. Kobe's highly **decorated** high school career made him the 13th overall choice by the Charlotte Hornets in the 1996 NBA draft.

科比·布莱恩特第一次关注篮球是在他上中学的时候。他在篮球方面很有天赋，费城的各所中学都密切关注着他的成长。这个六英尺高的七年级学生的确有打篮球的基因，因为他的爸爸是前 NBA 前锋乔·布莱恩特。科比在他父亲的关注下发展自己的篮球天赋，父亲帮助他成为了一名职业篮球运动员。他每天都练习篮球，看录像带，在操场上练习，听爸爸的建议。

当科比进入费城的一所大学时，他已是一个接受了很好训练的新人。他证明自己有成为下一届球星的技术和职业道德，并且球探也发现了这一点。科比没有让任何人失望，他在大学的第一年就加入了校队，尽管他不能一下子成为超级球星。无数个清晨在体育馆的训练使他的才华得到了进一步的提升。

科比在中学时就成为一名出色的球员了。不久，他又挖掘自己的潜力，使自己的水平又得到了提升。他在大学三年级和四年级期间每场比赛都备受关注并且没有让任何人失望。他曾经使学校体育馆挤满了人，这造成了学校外面主要高速公路的交通堵塞。

　　他继续完成他的大学学业，而此时他已经是宾夕法尼亚历史上创纪录的球员了，他的总分为 2 883 分。科比充满荣誉的大学生涯使他在 1996 年的 NBA 选秀中被夏洛特黄蜂队选中。

核心单词

dominate ['dɔmineit] *v.* 支配，统治，控制

gene [dʒiːn] *n.* 基因，遗传因子

mission ['miʃən] *n.* 外交使团；使命，任务

recruit [ri'kruːt] *v.* 征募；吸收

scout [skaut] *n.* 侦察者；侦察兵

escalate ['eskəleit] *v.* 提升；提高

decorate ['dəkəreit] *v.* 装饰，修饰

实用句型

He sold out the games everywhere he played during his junior and senior years and he didn't disappoint anyone.

他在大学三年级和四年级期间每场比赛都备受关注，并且没有让任何人失望。

①这里是 everywhere 引导的状语从句。

② sell out 卖光，类似的表达还有 sell up 卖掉等固定搭配。

翻译行不行

1. 他们两人之间逐渐产生了友情。(grow up)

....

2. 别担心，我决不会让你失望的。(let...down)

....

3. 这家商店的衬衫都卖光了。(sell out)

....

Forgiveness
宽 恕

To forgive may be **divine**, but no one ever said it was easy. When someone has deeply hurt you, it can be extremely difficult to let go of your grudge. But forgiveness is possible, and it can be surprisingly beneficial to your physical and mental health.

"People who forgive show less **depression**, anger and stress and more hopefulness," says Frederic, Ph.D., author of *Forgive for Good*, "So it can help save on the wear and tear on our organs, **reduce** the wearing out of the immune system and allow people to feel more vital."

So how do you start the healing? Try the following steps:

Calm yourself To defuse your anger, try a simple stress-management technique. "Take a couple of breaths and think of something that gives you pleasure: a beautiful scene in nature, or someone you love." Frederic says.

Don't wait for an apology "Many times the person who hurt you has no intention of apologizing," Frederic says, "they may have wanted to hurt you or they just don't see things the same way. So if you wait for people to apologize, you could be waiting an awfully long time." Keep in mind that forgiveness does not necessarily mean reconciliation with the person who upset you or condoning of his or her action.

Take the control away from your offender　Mentally replaying your hurt gives power to the person who caused you pain."Instead of focusing on your wounded feelings, learn to look for the love, beauty and kindness around you," Frederic says.

Try to see things from the other person's perspective　If you empathize with that person, you may realize that he or she was acting out of ignorance, fear, even love. To gain perspective, you may want to write a letter to yourself from your offender's point of view.

Recognize the benefits of forgiveness　Research has shown that people who forgive report more energy, better appetite and better sleep patterns.

Don't forget to forgive yourself　"For some people, forgiving themselves is the biggest **challenge**," Frederic says,"but it can rob you of your self-confidence if you don't do it."

兰　迪

　　宽恕或许是神圣的，但是，没有人认为宽恕是件容易的事。如果有人深深地伤害到你时，你很难做到不记恨于心。然而，如果心存宽恕，要做到这点就不难了，它会为你的身心健康带来意想不到的益处。

《宽恕的好处》的作者弗雷德里克博士说："怀有宽仁之心的人很少会沮丧、愤怒和压抑，他们更易满怀希望。由此看来，宽恕可以减少我们的疲惫和悲伤，能减轻免疫系统的疲劳，使人们更有活力。"

那么，该如何调整自己呢？试试下面的方法吧：

使自己冷静下来　试着以一种简单的压力管理方法来浇灭你的愤怒吧。弗雷德里克建议"做几次深呼吸，想一想能给你带来快乐的事物：自然界的美丽景色，或者是你深爱的人。"

不要期盼道歉　弗雷德里克说："很多时候，伤害你的人是不会向你道歉的。他们可能是有意伤害你。或者是他们看待问题的角度与你的截然相反。倘若你期盼他们的道歉，你会等待很长时间。"要记住，宽恕并不一定是与伤害你的人和好如初或原谅他（她）的行为。

将注意力从伤害你的人身上移开　总是想着自己的伤痛只会让自己更加痛苦。弗雷德里克说："你不应关注自己受伤的情绪，而应学会去寻找周围的爱、善、美。"

试着从别人的角度来考虑问题　如果你站在他（她）的角度，就会明白，他（她）那么做是出于无知、害怕，甚至是爱。换个角度，你可能想从伤害你的人的角度出发，给自己写封信。

认识宽恕的好处　研究表明，怀有宽恕之心的人精力更充沛，胃口和睡眠也更好。

不要忘记宽恕你自己　弗雷德里克说："对有些人来说，宽恕自己是最大的挑战。如果不宽恕自己，自信心便会受到打击。"

Practising
& Exercise

实战
提升篇

核心单词

divine [di'vain] *adj.* 神的；天赐的

depression [di'preʃən] *n.* 沮丧，意气消沉

reduce [ri'dju:s] *v.* 减少；降低

apology [ə'pɔlədʒi] *n.* 道歉；赔罪

mentally ['mentəli] *adv.* 心理上；精神上

perspective [pə'spektiv] *n.* 洞察力；展望，前途

offender [ə'fendə] *n.* 冒犯者；违法者

challenge ['tʃælindʒ] *n.* 挑战；质疑；指责

实用句型

Take the control away from your offender.

将注意力从伤害你的人身上移开。

①这是一个祈使句。

② take away 带走，拿走，类似的表达还有 take off 起飞；take up 开始从事等固定搭配。

翻译行不行

1. 就几天的时间。(a couple of)

....

2. 谁拿走了我的钢笔？(take away)

....

3. 当我情绪低落的时候，总是第一个想到你。(think of)

....

曾有一个人，**爱我**如生命

First love, forever love

I'll always Be There for You
我永远都会在你的身边

• Tracy Anderson •

No matter what happens, I'll always be there for you!

In 1989 an 8.2 earthquake almost **flattened** America, killing over 30,000 people in less than four minutes.

In the midst of utter devastation and **chaos**, a father left his wife safely at home and rushed to the school where his son was supposed to be, only to discover that the building was as flat as a pancake. After the unforgettably initial shock, he remembered the promise he had made to his son: "No matter what, I'll always be there for you!" And tears began to fill his eyes. As he looked at the pile of ruins that once was the school, it looked hopeless, but he kept remembering his **commitment** to his son.

He began to direct his attention towards where he walked his son to class at school each morning. Remembering his son's classroom would be in the back right corner of the building, he rushed there and started digging through the ruins.

As he was digging, other helpless parents arrived, clutching their hearts, saying: "My son!" "My daughter!"

Other well-meaning parents tried to pull him off what was left of the school, saying: "It's too late! They're all dead! You can't help! Go home! Come on, face **reality**, there's nothing you can do!" To each parent he responded with one line; "Are you going to help me now?" And then he continued to dig for his son, stone by stone.

The fire chief showed up and tried to pull him off the school's ruins saying, "Fires are breaking out, explosions are happening everywhere. You're in danger. We'll take care of it. Go home." To which this loving,caring American father asked,"Are you going to help me now?"

The police came and said, "You're angry, **anxious** and it's over. You're endangering others. Go home. We'll handle it!" To which he replied, "Are you going to help me now?" No one helped.

Courageously he went on alone because he needed to know for himself ; "Is my boy **alive** or is he dead?" He dug for eight hours. .. 12 hours. . . 24 hours. . . 36 hours. .. then, in the 38th hour, he pulled back a large stone and heard his son's voice.

He screamed his son's name, "ARMAND !"

He heard back, "Dad!?! It's me, Dad! I told the other kids not to worry. I told them that if you were alive, you'd save me and when you saved me, they'd be saved. You promised, no matter what happens, You'll always be there for me! You did it, Dad!"

"What's going on in there? How is it ?" the father asked.

"There are 14 of us left out of 33, Dad. We're **scared**, hungry, thirsty and thankful you're here. When the building collapsed, it made a **triangle**, and it saved us."

"Come out, boy!" "No, Dad! Let the other kids out first, because I know you'll get me! No matter what happens, I know you'll always be there for me!"

特雷西·安德森

不管发生什么，我永远都会在你的身边！

1989 年，一次 8.2 级的地震几乎铲平美国，在短短不到 4 分钟的时间里，夺去了 3 万多人的生命！

在彻底的破坏与混乱之中，有位父亲在安顿好他的妻子后，跑到他儿子就读的学校，而触目所见，却是被夷为平地的校园。看到这令人伤心的一幕，他想起了曾经对儿子所作的承诺："不论发生什么事，我都会在你身边。"至此，父亲热泪满眶。目睹曾经的学校成为了一堆瓦砾，真叫人绝望。但父亲仍然牢记着他对儿子的承诺。

他开始努力回忆每天早上送儿子上学的必经之路，终于记起儿子的教室应该就在那幢建筑物后面的右边的角落里，他跑到那儿，开始在碎石砾中挖掘。

当这位父亲正在挖掘时，其他束手无策的学生家长也赶到了现场，揪心地叫着："我的儿子呀！""我的女儿呀！"一些好意的家长试图把这位父亲劝离现场，告诉他"一切都太迟了！他们全死了！这样做没用的，回去吧，接受现实吧，你这样做一点用都没有。"面对种种劝告，这位父亲的回答只有一句话："你们愿意帮我吗？"然后继续一块一块地挖，在废墟中寻找着他的儿子。

消防队长来了，他也试图把这位父亲劝走，对他说："火灾频现，四处都有爆炸，你在这里太危险了，这边的事我们会处理，你回家吧！"对此，这位慈爱、关切的父亲仍然说："你们要帮我吗？"

警察赶到了现场并对他说："你现在又气又急，该结束了，你在危及他人，回家吧！我们会处理一切的。"这位父亲依旧是那句话："你们愿意帮我吗？"然而，人们无动于衷。

为了弄清楚儿子是死是活，这位父亲鼓起了勇气，独自一人继续挖掘。在挖掘了 8 小时，12 小时，24 小时，36 小时……38 小时后，父亲推开了一块巨大的石头，他听到了儿子的声音。

父亲大声地叫着："阿曼德！"

然后传来了儿子的回音："爸爸吗？是我，爸爸，我告诉其他的小朋友不要着急。我告诉他们如果你活着，你会来救我的。如果我获救了，他们也就获救了。你答应过我，不管发生什么，你永远都会在我的身边，你做到了，爸爸！"

"你那里的情况怎样？"父亲问。

"我们有 33 个，只有 14 个还活着。爸爸，我们好害怕，又渴又饿，谢天谢地，你在这儿。教室倒塌时，刚好形成一个三角形的洞，这个洞救了我们。"

"快出来吧！儿子！""不，爸爸，让其他小朋友先出去吧！因为我知道你会来接我的！不管发生什么事，我知道你永远都会在我的身边！"

核心单词

flatten ['flætn] *v.* 使平坦；弄平

chaos ['keiɔs] *n.* 混乱；杂乱的一团

commitment [kə'mitmənt] *n.* 托付，交托；委任

reality [ri(:)'æliti] *n.* 现实；真实

anxious ['æŋkʃəs] *adj.* 焦虑的，挂念的

alive [ə'laiv] *adj.* 活着的；现存的

scare [skɛə] *v.* 惊吓，使恐惧

triangle ['traiæŋgl] *n.* 三角板，三角尺

实用句型

No matter what happens，I'll always be there for you!

不管发生什么，我永远都会在你的身边！

①这里是 no matter 引导的让步状语从句。

②no matter 无论……，类似的表达还有 regardless of 不管，不顾等。

翻译行不行

1. 在逃亡期间，他在人迹罕至的旷野中走了 6 天。(in the midst of)

....

2. 谁能帮我照顾一下这个孩子呢？(take care of)

....

3. 他的新小说什么时候出版？(come out)

....

To Buy An Hour From Father
向爸爸买一个小时

A man came home from work late, tired and **irritated**, to find his 5-year-old son waiting for him at the door.

"Daddy, may I ask you a question?"

"Yeah, sure, what is it?" replied the man.

"Daddy, how much do you make an hour?"

"That's none of your business. Why do you ask such a thing?" the man said angrily. "I just want to know. Please tell me, how much do you make an hour?" **pleaded** the little boy.

"If you must know, I make $20 an hour."

"Oh," the little boy replied, with his head down. Looking up, he said, "Daddy, may I please borrow $10?"

The father was **furious**, "If the only reason you asked that is so you can borrow some money to buy a silly toy or some other nonsense, then you **march** yourself straight to your room and go to bed. Think about why you are being so selfish. I work hard everyday for this childish behavior."

The little boy quietly went to his room and shut the door. The man sat down and started to get even angrier about the little boy's questions. How dare he ask such questions only to get some money? After about an hour or so, the man had calmed down, and started to think: Maybe there was something he really needed to buy with that $10 and he really didn't ask for money very often.

The man went to the door of the little boy's room and opened the door.

"Are you asleep, son?" he asked.

"No, daddy, I'm awake," replied the boy.

"I've been thinking, maybe I was too hard on you earlier," said the man, "it's been a long day and I took out my aggravation on you. Here is the $10 you asked for."

The little boy sat straight up, smiling. "Oh, thank you daddy!" he **yelled**. Then, reaching under his pillow he pulled out some crumpled up bills. *The man, seeing that the boy already had money, started to get angry again.* The little boy slowly counted out his money, then looked up at his father.

"Why do you want more money if you already have some?" the father **grumbled**.

"Because I didn't have enough, but now I do," the little boy replied. "Daddy, I have $20 now. Can I buy an hour of your time? Please come home early tomorrow. I would like to have dinner with you."

塞缪尔

男人带着一身的疲倦，恼火地回到家，这时天色已晚，他发现 5 岁的儿子在门口等着他。

"爸爸，可以问你个问题吗？"

"当然可以，想问什么？"男人答道。

"你一个小时能赚多少钱？"

"这不关你的事。为什么问这个？"男人生气了。"我只是想知道。请你告诉我，你一个小时赚多少钱？"小男孩哀求道。

"如果非要知道的话，告诉你，我一小时赚 20 美元。"

"哦，"小男孩的头低下了，然后又抬起，说道："爸爸，我可以向你借 10 美元吗？"

男人暴怒，"如果你问这个问题，只是为了借钱买个愚蠢的玩具或一堆废品，那你趁早滚回房间睡觉去。好好想想你这种自私的行为！我每天辛辛苦苦地工作，难道就是为了你这种幼稚的行为吗？"

小男孩默默地回到房里，关上门。这时男人坐下来，想到刚才的提问感到更加恼怒。为什么他为了借钱胆敢问出这种问题？大约一个小时后，男人平静下来，开始想：或许他真的需要 10 美元买东西呢？他可是很少开口要钱的。

男人走到小男孩房门前，打开了门。

"睡了吗，儿子？"男人问道。

"没有呢，爸爸。"男孩答道。

"我一直在想，可能我刚才对你太过分了，"男人说，"爸爸工作一天太累了，所以把火都撒在你身上了。这是你要的 10 美元。"

　　小男孩顿时坐了起来，兴奋地叫道："谢谢，老爸！"然后，他把手伸到枕头底下，摸出一叠皱巴巴的钞票。男人看到男孩手里攥着一把钱，又生气了。小男孩慢慢地数着钱，然后抬头望着父亲。

　　"你自己有钱，为什么还跟我要钱？"父亲抱怨道。

　　"因为我的钱不够，但现在够了。"小男孩答道。"爸爸，我现在有 20 美元。我能向您买一个小时的时间吗？明天请早点回家，我想和您一起吃晚饭。"

Practising
& Exercise

实战提升篇

核心单词

irritate ['iriteit] *v.* 使恼怒；使烦躁

plead [pli:d] *v.* 辩护；以……为理由

furious ['fjuəriəs] *adj.* 狂怒的；强烈的

march [mɑ:tʃ] *n.* 行进；行军；行程

yell [jel] *v.* 叫喊；吼叫

grumble ['grʌmbl] *v.* 抱怨，发牢骚

实用句型

The man，seeing that the boy already had money，started to get angry again.

男人看到男孩手里攥着一把钱，又生气了。

①现在分词 seeing 在这里作状语。

②start 开始，另外还有 start up 突然出现；start off 出发，开始等固定搭配。

翻译行不行

1. 你认为那部影片怎么样？（think about）

....

2. 刚才哭闹的小孩一会就安静下来了。（calm down）

....

3. 门口有一位老人找你。（ask for）

....

A Letter to My Daughters
写给女儿的信

· Barack Obama ·

Dear Malia and Sasha,

   I know that you've both had a lot of fun these last two years on the campaign trail, going to picnics and **parades** and state fairs, eating all sorts of junk food your mother and I probably shouldn't have let you have. But I also know that it hasn't always been easy for you and Mom, and that as **excited** as you both are about that new puppy, it doesn't make up for all the time we've been apart. I know how much I've missed these past two years, and today I want to tell you a little more about why I decided to take our family on this journey.

   When I was a young man, I thought life was all about me—about how I'd make my way in the world, become successful, and get the things I want. But then the two of you came into my world with all your **curiosity** and mischief and those smiles that never fail to fill my heart and light up my day. And suddenly, all my big plans for myself didn't seem so important anymore. I soon found that the greatest joy in my life was the joy I saw in yours. *And I realized that my own life wouldn't count for much unless I was able to ensure that you had every opportunity for happiness and fulfillment in yours.* In the end, girls, that's why I ran for President: because of what I want for you and for every child in this nation.

I want all our children to go to schools worthy of their **potential**—schools that challenge them, inspire them, and instill in them a sense of wonder about the world around them. I want them to have the chance to go to college—even if their parents aren't rich. And I want them to get good jobs: jobs that pay well and give them benefits like health care, jobs that let them spend time with their own kids and retire with dignity.

I want us to push the boundaries of discovery so that you'll live to see new technologies and inventions that improve our lives and make our planet cleaner and safer. And I want us to push our own human boundaries to reach beyond the divides of race and region, gender and religion that keep us from seeing the best in each other.

Sometimes we have to send our young men and women into war and other **dangerous** situations to protect our country—but when we do, I want to make sure that it is only for a very good reason, that we try our best to settle our differences with others peacefully, and that we do everything possible to keep our servicemen and women safe. And I want every child to understand that the **blessings** these brave Americans fight for are not free—that with the great privilege of being a citizen of this nation comes great responsibility.

That was the lesson your grandmother tried to teach me when I was your age, reading me the opening lines of the *Declaration of Independence* and telling me about the men and women who marched for **equality** because they believed those words put to paper two centuries ago should mean something.

She helped me understand that America is great not because it is perfect but because it can always be made better, and that the unfinished work of perfecting our union falls to each of us. It's a charge we pass on to our children, coming closer with each new generation to what we know America should be.

I hope both of you will take up that work, righting the wrongs that you see and working to give others the chances you've had. Not just because you have an **obligation** to give something back to this country that has given our family so much—although you do have that obligation. But because you have an obligation to yourself. Because it is only when you hitch your wagon to something larger than yourself that you will realize your true potential.

These are the things I want for you—to grow up in a world with no limits on your dreams and no achievements beyond your reach, and to grow into compassionate, committed women who will help build that world. And I want every child to have the same chances to learn and dream and grow and thrive that you girls have. That's why I've taken our family on this great adventure.

I am so proud of both of you. I love you more than you can ever know. And I am grateful every day for your patience, poise, grace, and humor as we prepare to start our new life together in the White House.

Love, Dad

巴拉克·奥巴马

亲爱的玛莉亚和莎夏：

我知道这两年你们俩随我一路竞选都有过不少乐子，野餐、游行、逛州博览会，吃了各种或许我和你妈不该让你们吃的垃圾食物。然而我也知道，你们俩和你妈的日子，有时候并不是那么惬意。新来的小狗虽然令你们兴奋，却无法弥补我们不在一起的时光。我明白这两年我错过的太多了，今天我要再向你们说说为什么我决定带领我们一家走上这条路。

在我年轻的时候，我认为生活就该围着我转：我如何在这世上得心应手，成功立业，得到我想要的。后来，你们俩进入了我的世界，带来了种种好奇、淘气和微笑，这些总能填满我的心，照亮我的生活。突然之间，我为自己谱写的伟大计划显得不再那么重要了。我很快便发现，我在你们生命中看到的快乐，也是我自己生命中最大的快乐。而我同时也意识到，如果我不能确保你们此生能够拥有追求幸福和自我实现的一切机会，我自己的生命也就没有多大价值。总而言之，我的女儿，这就是我竞选总统的原因：我要让你们俩和这个国家的每一个孩子，都能拥有我想给你们的东西。

我要让所有孩子都在能够发掘他们潜能的学校就读；这些学校要能挑战他们，激励他们，并灌输给他们对这个世界的好奇心。我要他们都有机会上大学——哪怕他们的父母并不富有。而且，我要他们都能找到好的工作：薪酬高还附带健康保险的工作，让他们有时间陪孩子，并且能过上有尊严的退休生活。

我要大家向发现的极限挑战，让你们在有生之年能够看见改善我们生活、使这个行星更干净、更安全的高科技和新发明。我也要大家向自己的人际界限挑战，跨越使我们看不到对方长处的种族、地域、性别和宗教的樊篱。

有时候为了保护我们的国家，我们不得不把青年男女派到战场或其他危险的地方——然而当我们这么做的时候，我要确保师出有名，我们尽全力以和平的方式化解与他人的争执，也想尽一切办法保障男女官兵的安全。我想要每个孩子都明白，这些勇敢的美国人在战场上捍卫的福祉是无法平白得到的——在享有作为这个国家公民的伟大特权之际，重责大任也随之而来。

这正是我在你们这么大时，你们的祖母教给我的，她把《独立宣言》开头几行念给我听，告诉我有一些男女为了争取平等而游行抗议，因为他们认为两个世纪前白纸黑字写下来的这些句子，不应该只是空话。

她让我了解到，美国之所以伟大，不是因为它完美，而是因为我们可以不断地让它变得更好，而让它变得更好的使命，就落在了我们每个人的身上。这是我们交给孩子们的任务，每过一代，美国就更接近我们的理想。

我希望你们俩都愿意接下这个工作，看到不对的事要想办法改正，努力帮助别人获得你们有过的机会。这并非只因国家给了我们一家人这么多，你们也当有所回馈。这不仅因为你们对国家有这个义务，而且你们对自己也有这个义务。因为，唯有在把你的马车套在更大的东西上时，你才会明白自己真正的潜能有多大。

　　这些是我想要让你们得到的东西——在一个梦想不受限制、无事不能成就的世界中长大，长成具有慈悲心且坚持理想，能帮忙打造那样一个世界的女性。我要每个孩子都有和你们一样的机会，去学习、梦想、成长和发展。这就是我带领我们一家展开这个大冒险的原因。

　　我深以你们俩为荣，你们永远不会明白我有多爱你们，在我们准备在白宫开始新生活之际，我没有一天不为你们的忍耐、沉稳、明理和幽默而心存感激。

爱你们的老爸

Practising

实战 提升篇

& Exercise

核心单词

parade [pəˈreid] *n.* 行进，游行 *v.* 在……游行

excited [ikˈsaitid] *adj.* 兴奋的；激动的

curiosity [ˌkjuəriˈɔsiti] *n.* 好奇心；奇品

potential [pəˈtenʃ(ə)l] *adj.* 潜在的，可能的

dangerous [ˈdeindʒrəs] *adj.* 危险的；不安全的

blessing [ˈblesiŋ] *n.* (上帝的) 赐福；祝福

equality [i(ː)ˈkwɔliti] *n.* 相等；平等

obligation [ˌɔbliˈgeiʃen] *n.* 义务；责任

实用句型

And I realized that my own life wouldn't count for much unless I was able to ensure that you had every opportunity for happiness and fulfillment in yours.

我同时也意识到，如果我不能确保你们此生能够拥有追求幸福和自我实现的一切机会，我自己的生命也就没有多大价值。

①that 在这里引导宾语从句。

②count for 值，计，类似的表达还有 count on 依靠，指望；count in 把……算入等固定搭配。

翻译行不行

1. 太阳照亮了天空和大地。(light up)

....

2. 你必须把时间和地点弄清楚。(make sure)

....

3. 他是什么时候开始踢足球的？(take up)

....

Memo from A Child to Parents
孩子给爸爸妈妈的备忘录

· Brandon ·

1. Don't spoil me. I know quite well that I ought not to have all I ask for. I'm only testing you.

2. Don't be afraid to be firm with me. I prefer it, it makes me feel **secure**.

3. Don't let me form bad habits. I have to rely on you to detect them in the early stages.

4. Don't make me feel smaller than I am. It only makes me behave **stupidly** "big".

5. Don't correct me in front of people if you can help it. *I'll take much more notice if you talk quietly with me in private*.

6. Don't make me feel that my mistakes are sins. It upsets my sense of values.

7. Don't protect me from consequences. I need to learn the painful way sometimes.

8. Don't be too upset when I say "I hate you". Sometimes it isn't you I hate but your power to **thwart** me.

9. Don't take too much notice of my small ailments. Sometimes they get me the attention I need.

10. Don't nag. If you do, I shall have to protect myself by appearing deaf.

11. Don't forget that I cannot explain myself as well as I should like. That is why I am not always **accurate**.

12. Don't put me off when I ask questions. If you do, you will find that I stop asking and seek my information elsewhere.

13. Don't be inconsistent. That completely **confuses** me and makes me lose faith in you.

14. Don't tell me my fears are silly. They are terribly real and you can do much to reassure me if you try to understand.

15. Don't ever suggest that you are perfect or infallible. It gives me too great a shock when I discover that you are neither.

16. Don't ever think that it is beneath your dignity to apologize to me. An honest apology makes me feel surprisingly warm towards you.

17. Don't forget I love experimenting. I couldn't get along without it, so please put up with it.

18. Don't forget how quickly I am growing up. It must be very difficult for you to keep pace with me, but please do try.

19. Don't forget that I don't **thrive** without lots of love and understanding, but I don't need to tell you, do I?

20. Please keep yourself fit and **healthy**. I need you.

1. 不要娇惯我。我很明白，不是我要什么就能得到什么的。有时我只是在试探你们。

2. 不要害怕在我面前坚持你们的立场。我其实更喜欢你们这样，因为这让我有安全感。

3. 不要让我养成坏习惯。只有你们才能把它们消灭在萌芽状态。

4. 不要让我感觉自己比实际要小，那样只能使我愚蠢地去充"大"个。

5. 如果有可能，不要当众教训我。如果你们在私底下跟我说，我会更加注意的。

6. 不要让我感觉自己犯了错误就像犯了罪一样，那只能搞乱我的价值观。

7. 不要阻止我承担后果，有时我需要吸取教训。

8. 当我说"我恨你"时，请不要生气。有时我恨的不是你们，我恨的只是你们那令我感到很渺小的权威。

9. 我得了小病时，不要太在意我。有时生病可以使我得到我所需要的关注。

10. 不要唠唠叨叨的。如果你们啰嗦的话，我只能通过装聋作哑来保护自己。

11. 不要忘记，有时我会词不达意。这也是为什么我有时不能准确地表达自己的原因。

12. 当我问问题时，不要不耐烦。否则，你们会发现我不再问你们问题，而是从别的地方寻找答案。

13. 不要出尔反尔，这样只能令我疑惑，并对你们失去信任。

14. 不要对我说我的恐惧是可笑的。它们是真真实实的，如果你们能理解我，你们就能更好地安慰我。

15. 永远不要暗示你们是完美的或是不会犯错误的。否则当我发现事实与此相反时，我会感到很震惊的。

16. 永远不要认为向我道歉有损于你们的尊严。一个诚实的道歉会让我感到非常地温暖。

17. 不要忘了我喜欢尝试。如果我不尝试就寸步难行，所以请你们包容。

18. 不要忘了我长得很快。你们肯定觉得与我俱进是非常困难的，但是还是请你们努力去做。

19. 不要忘了离开了厚爱和理解，我就不会茁壮成长。但是，这一点我不需要提醒你们吧？

20. 请保持身体健康，因为我需要你们。

核心单词

secure [si'kjuə] *adj.* 安全的；无忧虑的

stupidly ['stju:pidli] *adv.* 愚蠢地

thwart [θwɔ:t] *v.* 反对，阻挠

accurate ['ækjurit] *adj.* 准确的；精确的

confuse [kən'fju:z] *v.* 把……弄糊涂，使困惑

thrive [θraiv] *v.* 兴旺，繁荣；成功

healthy ['helθi] *adj.* 健康的；健全的

实用句型

I'll take much more notice if you talk quietly with me in private.

如果你们在私底下跟我说，我会更加注意的。

① if 在这里引导条件状语从句。

② in private 私下，秘密地，类似的表达还有 in public 公开地等。

翻译行不行

1. 这天气可靠不住。(rely on)

....

2. 今天能做的事不要拖到明天再做。(put off)

....

3. 他学习的进展如何？(get along)

....

Extra Good Luck

好运符——一张两美元钞票

· Derek ·

I keep a two-dollar bill in my wallet that was given to me by my mother when I was six years old.

I am not **superstitious** but the bill goes with me wherever I go. My mother gave it to me so that luck would follow me everywhere.

She looked at me and said, "I want you to carry this two dollar bill for extra good luck."

"Thanks mom," I replied, "I will keep it close to me always."

Every morning I would get dressed and my two-dollar bill went into my pocket. My mother passed away when I was 17 years old and I remembered taking out my two dollar bill. I held it in my hand for the longest time and knew that she would be watching over me the rest of my life.

Each time I felt I had a crisis on my hands, I could reach for my two dollar bill and set it on the table. I would stare at it for several hours and could always come up with a solution.

When I applied for my first job, I was thirty years old and

very shy. The thought of being interviewed for a job was **scary** but I had to work. *On my first interview, as I sat in the waiting room, I noticed there were five women ahead of me.* All of the women were younger and very well dressed. One of them was **impeccable** in her blue striped suit with matching purse and shoes. I knew I was up against women better qualified by looking at the length of their resumes.

Ms Martin, the office manager, summoned me into her office.

"What makes you feel you are **qualified** for this job?" she asked.

"I really need this job and there is nothing I can not do." I responded.

She asked me a series of questions and the interview was over. As I exited her office, I turned around and said, "Ms Martin, I know that 1 am not qualified like your other applicants, but please give me a chance. I learn quickly and can be a very productive member of your team."

I thanked her and went home **exhausted**. Oh well, I thought, tomorrow would be another day.

That evening as I was getting ready for bed, I received a phone call from Ms Martin.

"Gina," she said, "you were not the most qualified **applicant**, but you have so much confidence in yourself that we decided to give you a chance to prove yourself."

I screamed out loud, was jumping all over the room in disbelief. I could hear Ms Martin laughing in the background and suddenly I realized that Ms Martin was still on the line.

"Thank you, Ms Martin, you will not regret this decision." I said and hung up the phone.

I got my wallet and took out my two-dollar bill.

"Thanks mom, I am going to make it." I said out loud so my mother could hear me.

At that instant, I remembered the time she pulled all of us into the living room and said, "You are all brilliant in my mind, but if you fail once don't give up. Don't fear failure. It is a way of getting us to try harder. You will succeed, I promise."

I still think of mom every day and still keep my two-dollar bill in my wallet. At a family reunion years later, I found out that my brothers and sisters all had a two-dollar bill in their wallet.

We all laughed and talked about how **special** this gift from mom had been to each and ever had reinforced the confidence mom had instilled one of us. It led in us.

德里克

在我的钱夹里一直保存着一张两美元的钞票，那是我 6 岁时妈妈给的。

我不迷信，但无论到哪里，我都随身带着它。妈妈希望这张两美元钞票能让我事事顺利。

当时，她看着我说："带上这两美元吧，它会带给你好运。"

"谢谢妈妈，"我说，"我会永远带着它。"

每天早上，穿好衣服后，我就将它装进口袋。17岁那年，妈妈去世了。当时，我掏出那张两美元钞票，久久地攥在手中。我知道，妈妈会一直关注我以后的生活。

每每遇到棘手问题，我就拿出那张钞票，放在桌上，一连几个小时盯着它，最终总能想出解决的办法。

第一次找工作时我已经30岁了，又有些羞怯。一想到要面试，我就很害怕，但我必须得工作。第一次面试时，在等候室里，除了我还有五位女性求职者。她们都比我年轻，并且衣着考究。其中一位穿着蓝色条纹套装，配以类似风格的钱包和鞋子，简直太完美了。我很清楚，光看履历，我就不是这五位女士的对手了。

业务经理马丁太太把我叫进办公室。

"你觉得你能胜任这份工作的理由是什么？"她问道。

"我很需要这份工作，而且，也没有我做不来的事。"我答道。

回答完一连串的问题后，面试结束了。在我迈出办公室前，我转身对马丁太太说："马丁太太，我知道自己并不如其他人优秀，但是，请您给我一个机会。我接受能力很强，会成为公司优秀的一员。"

谢过马丁太太，等回到家时，我已经疲惫不堪了。我想：算了，没有关系，明天又是新的一天。

当晚，我正准备睡觉时，突然接到马丁太太的电话。

"吉娜，"她说，"你虽不是应试者中最出色的，但你对自己充满信心，因此我们决定给你一个展现自己的机会。"

我简直难以相信这是真的，我激动得大叫起来，兴奋地在房间里又蹦又跳。电话那头传来马丁太太的笑声，我这才意识到电话还没挂。

"马丁太太，谢谢您！我不会让您失望的。"说完，我挂断了电话。

我掏出钱夹，拿出了那张两美元的钞票。

"谢谢您，妈妈，我的好运来了。"我大声地说，妈妈应该听得到。

那一刻，我想起了妈妈说的一番话，她把我们拉到客厅里说："在妈妈眼里，你们都很棒。无论做什么事情，失败了，千万别放弃。失败并不可怕，我们可以化失败为动力。我相信，你们一定能够成功。"

我时刻都想念着妈妈，那两美元也依然珍藏在我的钱夹里。多年后，在一次家庭聚会上，我才发现，我们兄弟姐妹的钱夹里都各有一张两美元的钞票。

我们都笑了，谈论着妈妈赠予我们的这份特殊礼物。她在我们心底播下了自信的种子，而这两美元让这粒种子迅速茁壮地成长起来。

Practising
& Exercise

核心单词

superstitious [ˌsjuːpəˈstiʃəs] *adj.* 迷信的

scary [ˈskɛəri] *adj.* 胆小的；提心吊胆的

impeccable [imˈpekəbl] *adj.* 无懈可击的；无缺点的

qualify [ˈkwɔlifai] *v.* 使具有资格，使合格

exhausted [igˈzɔːstid] *adj.* 耗尽的，用完的

applicant [ˈæplikənt] *n.* 申请人

special [ˈspeʃəl] *adj.* 特别的，特殊的

实用句型

On my first interview，as I sat in the waiting room，I noticed there were five women ahead of me.

第一次面试时，在等候室里，除了我还有五位女性求职者。

①这里是由 as 引导的时间状语从句。

②ahead of 在 ... 之前，类似的表达还有 go ahead 先走等。

翻译行不行

1. 会议上提出了许多问题。（come up）

....

2. 他申请休假。（applied for）

....

3. 我真希望自己能戒酒。（give up）

....

Mother's Hands
妈妈的手

• Louisa Godissart McQuillen •

Night after night, she came to **tuck** me in, even long after my childhood years. Following her longstanding **custom**, she'd lean down and push my long hair out of the way, then kiss my forehead.

I don't remember when it first started annoying me— her hands pushing my hair that way. But it did annoy me, for they felt work-worn and rough against my young skin. Finally, one night, I lashed out at her: "Don't do that anymore—your hands are too rough!" She didn't say anything in reply. But never again did my mother close out my day with that familiar expression of her love. Lying awake long afterward, my words **haunted** me. But pride stifled my conscience, and I didn't tell her I was sorry.

Time after time, with the passing years, my thoughts returned to that night. By then I missed my mother's hands, missed her goodnight kiss upon my forehead. Sometimes the incident seemed very close, sometimes far away. But always it lurked, hauntingly, in the back of my mind.

Well, the years have passed, and I'm not a little girl anymore. Mom is in her mid-seventies, and those hands I once thought to be so rough are still doing things for me and my family. She's been our doctor, reaching into a medicine cabinet for the **remedy** to calm a young girl's stomach or **soothe** a boy's scraped knee. She cooks the best fried chicken in the world... gets stains out of blue jeans like I never could...and still insists on dishing out ice cream at any hour of the day or night.

Through the years, my mother's hands have put in countless hours of toil, and most of hers were before automatic washers!

Now, my own children are grown and gone. Mom no longer has Dad, and on special occasions, I find myself drawn next door to spend the night with her. So it was that late on Thanksgiving Eve, as I drifted into sleep in the bedroom of my youth, a familiar hand hesitantly stole across my face to brush the hair from my forehead. Then a kiss, ever so gently, touched my brow.

In my memory, for the thousandth time, I recalled the night my **surly** young voice complained: "Don't do that anymore—your hands are too rough!" Catching Mom's hand in my hand, I blurted out how sorry I was for that night. I thought she'd remember, as I did. But Mom didn't know what I was talking about. She had forgotten—and forgiven—long ago.

That night, I fell asleep with a new appreciation for my gentle mother and her caring hands. *And the guilt I had carried around for so long was nowhere to be found.*

路易莎·岗得萨特·麦克奎林

夜复一夜，她总是来帮我盖被子，即使我早已长大成人。这是妈妈的长期习惯，她总是弯下身来，拨开我的长发，在我的额上一吻。

不知从何时起，她拨开我头发的举动令我非常地不耐烦。但的确，我讨厌她因长期操劳而变得粗糙的手摩擦我细嫩的皮肤。最后，一天晚上，我冲她吼道："别再这样了——你的手太粗糙了！"她什么也没说。但妈妈再也没有这样表达过她的爱。直到很久以后，我还是常想起我的那些话。但自尊占了上风，我没有告诉妈妈我很后悔。

时光流逝，我又想到了那个晚上。那时我想念妈妈的手，想念她晚上在我额上的一吻。有时这幕情景似乎很近，有时又似乎很遥远。但它总是潜伏着，时常浮现，出现在我的意识中。

一年年过去，我也不再是小女孩，妈妈也有 70 多岁了。那双我认为很粗糙的手依然为我和我的家庭忙碌着。她是我家的医生，为我女儿在药橱里找胃药或在我儿子擦伤的膝盖上敷药。她能烧出世界上最美味的鸡…… 将牛仔裤弄干净而我却永远不能……而且在任何时候都能盛出冰激凌。

这么多年来，妈妈的手做了多少家务！而且在自动洗衣机出现以前她已经操劳了好长时间。

现在，我的孩子都已经长大，离开了家。爸爸去世了，有些时候，我睡在妈妈的隔壁房间。一次感恩节前夕的深夜，我睡在年轻时的卧室里，一只熟悉的手有些犹豫地、悄悄地掠过我的脸，从我额头上拨开头发，然后一个吻，轻轻地印在我的眉毛上。

在我的记忆中，无数次，想起那晚我粗暴、年轻的声音："别再这样了——你的手太粗糙了！"我抓住妈妈的手，对那晚的后悔之情脱口而出。我以为她想起来了，像我一样。但妈妈却不知道我在说些什么。她已经在很久以前就忘了这事，并早已原谅了我。

那晚，我带着对温柔母亲和她体贴双手的感激入睡。多年来我的负罪感在此刻已经消失无踪了。

Practising

& Exercise

实战
提升篇

核心单词

tuck [tʌk] *v.* 把……塞进，把……藏入

custom ['kʌstəm] *n.* 习俗，惯例

haunt [hɔ:nt] *v.* 萦绕在……心头；使困扰

remedy ['remidi] *n.* 治疗；治疗法；药物

soothe [su:ð] *v.* 安慰；使平静

surely ['ʃuəli] *adv.* 确实，无疑，--定

实用句型

And the guilt I had carried around for so long was nowhere to be found.

多年来我的负罪感在此刻已经消失无踪了。

① guilt 后省略了 that。

② nowhere 任何地方都不，类似的词还有 noway；nowise 等。

翻译行不行

1. 他们猛烈抨击大学的招生制度。(lash out)

....

2. 我仍坚持我的观点。(insist on)

....

3. 如果没有重力，我们就无法平稳在站在地面上。(no longer)

....

A Dance with Dad
与父亲共舞

• Alan •

I am dancing with my father at my parents' 50th-wedding-anniver-sary celebration. The band is playing an old-fashioned waltz as we move gracefully across the floor. His hand on my **waist** is as guiding as it always was, and he hums the tune to himself in a steady, youthful way. Around and around we go, laughing and nodding to the other dancers.

We are the best dancers on the floor-they tell us. My father **squeezes** my hand and smiles at me. All the years that I refused to dance with him melt away now. And those early times come back.

I remember when I was almost three and my father came home from work, swooped me into his arms and began to dance me around the table. My mother laughed at us, told us dinner would get cold. But my father said, "She's just caught the **rhythm** of the dance! Our dinner can wait." Then he sang out, "Roll out the barrel, let's have a **barrel** of fun," and I sang back, "Let's get those blues on the run."

We danced through the years. One night when I was 15,

lost in some painful, **adolescent** mood. My father put on a stack of records and teased me to dance with him. "C'mon," he said, "let's get those blues on the run."

When I turned away from him, my father put his hand on my shoulder, and I jumped out of the chair screaming, "Don't touch me! I am sick and tired of dancing with you!" I saw the hurt on his face, but the words were out and I could not call them back. I ran to my room **sobbing** hysterically.

We did not dance together after that night. I found other partners, and my father waited up for me after dances, sitting in his **favorite** chair. Sometimes he would be asleep when I came in, and I would wake him, saying, "If you were so tired, you should have gone to bed."

"No, no," he'd say, "I was just waiting for you."

Then we'd lock up the house and go to bed.

My father waited up for me through my high school and college years when I danced my way out of his life.

Shortly after my first child was born; my mother called to tell me my father was ill. "A heart problem," she said, "now, don't come. It's three hundred miles. It would upset your father."

A proper diet restored him to good health. My mother wrote that they had joined a dance club. "The doctor says it's good exercise. You remember how your father loves to dance."

Yes, I remembered. My eyes filled up with remembering.

When my father **retired**, we mended our way back together again; hugs and kisses were common when we visited each other. He danced with the grandchildren, but he did not ask me to dance. I knew he was waiting for an apology from me. I could never find the right words.

As my parents' 50th anniversary approached, my brothers and I met to plan the party. My older brother said, "Do you remember that night you wouldn't dance with him? Boy, was he mad? I couldn't believe he'd get so mad about a thing like that. I'll bet you haven't danced with him since."

I did not tell him he was right.

My younger brother promised to get the band. "Make sure they can play waltzes and polkas," I told him.

I did not tell him that all I wanted to do was dance once more with my father.

When the band began to play after dinner, my parents took the floor. They glided around the room, inviting the others to join them. The guests rose to their feet, **applauding** the golden couple. My father danced with his granddaughters, and then the band began to play the "Beer Barrel Polka".

"Roll out the barrel," I heard my father singing. Then I knew it was time. I wound my way through a few couples and tapped my daughter on the shoulder.

"Excuse me," I said, looking directly into my father's eyes and almost choking on my words, "but I believe this is my dance."

My father stood rooted to the spot. Our eyes met and traveled back to that night when I was 15. In a **trembling** voice, I sang, "Let's get those blues on the run."

My father bowed and said, "Oh, yes. I've been waiting for you."

Then he started to laugh, and we moved into each other's arms.

艾 伦

在父母金婚纪念庆典上，伴着古老的华尔兹旋律，我与父亲在舞池中优雅地翩翩起舞。他从容地哼着轻快的乐曲，他把手放在我的腰际，引领着舞步。我们旋转着四处滑动，笑着对其他舞者点头致意。

大家都说，我和父亲是舞场中跳得最好的一对。父亲紧抓着我的手，微笑地望着我。许多年前，我曾拒绝和他跳舞，那道隔膜直到现在才消失殆尽，我们再次拥有了最初的美好时光。

记得在我大约 3 岁时，父亲下班回家总要猛地把我抱进怀里，然后开始围着餐桌跳舞。妈妈就会笑着说，晚饭都要凉了。可父亲说："她刚刚跟上节奏，过一会儿吃。"然后便唱了起来，"把桶滚出来，让我们拥有一个快乐的桶。"我也回唱着，"让我们滚走忧伤。"

很多年过去了，我们就这样跳着，直到我 15 岁的一个晚上，我沉浸在青春期莫名的悲伤中，父亲拿出一摞唱片，揶揄着让我跟他跳舞，"来吧，"他说，"让我们滚走忧伤。"

我转过身去，父亲将手放到我的肩上，我腾地从椅子上跳起来，朝他尖叫道："不准碰我，我不想和你跳舞！"我看见他脸上流露出受伤的神情，但话已出口，无法收回。我跑回卧室，大哭了起来。

从那以后，我们再也没有一起跳过舞。我有了其他的舞伴，而父亲总是坐在他最喜欢的椅子上等着我跳完回来。有时候，我回来时他已经睡着了，我叫醒他说，"你要是太累，就上床去睡吧。"

"不，不累，"他总说，"我只是在等你。"

然后，我们便各自关上房门，上床睡觉。

整个高中和大学期间，当我跳出他的生命，用自己的方式舞蹈时。他就这样等着我。

我生下第一个孩子不久，妈妈打电话告诉我，爸爸病了。"心脏问题，"她说，"你现在别回来，300英里远的路，会让你爸爸不安的。"

合理饮食帮助父亲恢复了健康。妈妈来信说，他们参加了一个舞蹈俱乐部，"医生说这是种很好的运动，你还记得，你爸爸曾经多么喜欢跳舞吧。"

是的，我记得，眼里满是回忆。

父亲退休后，我们努力想让彼此的关系回到从前，每次见面时，我们会拥抱和亲吻对方。他和孙儿们跳舞，但从不邀请我。我知道他是在等我道歉，但我总也说不出口。

父母金婚纪念日快到时，我和兄弟们商量宴会事宜。哥哥说："你还记得那晚拒绝和他跳舞吗？爸爸真疯狂。真不敢相信他这么迷恋跳舞。我打赌，从那以后你再没和他跳过舞。"

他说对了，但我没说话。

弟弟说他去找乐队，我对他说，"一定要找能演奏华尔兹和波尔卡的乐队。"

我没告诉他，我只是希望能与父亲再跳一次舞。

晚饭后，乐队开始演奏，父母进入舞池，并邀请其他客人加入。他们在房间四周慢慢滑动舞步，大家都站了起来，为金婚夫妻鼓掌祝贺。在父亲与孙女们跳舞时，乐队开始演奏起了"啤酒桶波尔卡"。

"把桶滚出来，"我听到父亲轻轻哼唱着。是时候了，我绕过几对夫妇，拍了拍女儿的肩膀。

"对不起，"我直视父亲的眼睛，几乎说不出话来，"我想该轮到我了。"

父亲一动不动地站在那里。我们对视着，似乎又回到了我15岁的那个夜晚。我的声音颤抖着，唱道，"让我们滚走忧伤。"

父亲弯下腰来，说道："噢，是的，我一直在等你。"

然后他开始笑起来，我们拥抱在一起。

核心单词

waist [weist] *n.* 腰，腰部

squeeze [skwi:z] *v.* 榨，挤，压

rhythm ['riðəm] *n.* 节奏；韵律

barrel ['bærəl] *n.* 大桶；一桶的量

adolescent [ˌædəu'lesnt] *n.* 青少年 *adj.* 青春期的

sobbing ['sɔbiŋ] *adj.* 湿透的

favorite ['feivərit] *adj.* 特别喜爱的

retired [ri'taiəd] *adj.* 引退的，退隐的；

applaud [ə'plɔːd] *v.* 向……鼓掌；向……喝彩

tremble ['trembl] *v.* 发抖；震颤

实用句型

I did not tell him that all I wanted to do was dance once more with my father. 我没告诉他，我只是希望能与父亲再跳一次舞。

① that 在这里引导宾语从句。

② once more 再一次，类似的表达还有 once again 等。

翻译行不行

1. 短裙子又开始流行了。(come back)

....

2. 我们去那家咖啡馆喝咖啡吧。(resort to)

....

3. 请填写这份调查表。(fill up)

....

Love Notes
爱的小纸条

It's been over eleven years now. It was a **wintry** afternoon, the snow swirling around the cedar trees outside, forcing little icicles to form at the tips of the deep green foliage clinging to the branches.

My older son, Stephen, was at school, and Reed, my husband, at work. My three little ones were **clustered** around the kitchen counter, the tabletop piled high with crayons and markers. Tom was perfecting a paper airplane, creating his own insignia with stars and stripes, while Sam worked on a self-portrait, his chubby hands drawing first a head, then legs and arms sticking out where the body should have been. The children mostly concentrated on their work. Tom occasionally tutoring his younger brother on exactly how to make a plane that would fly the entire length of the room.

But Laura, our only daughter, sat quietly, **engrossed** in her project. Every once in a while she would ask how to spell the name of someone in our family, then painstakingly form the letters one by one. Next, she would add flowers with small green stems, complete with grass lining the bottom of the page. She finished off each with a sun in the upper right hand corner, surrounded by an inch or two of blue sky. Holding them at eye level, she let out a long sigh of satisfaction.

"What are you making. Honey?" I asked.

She glanced at her brothers before looking back at me:

"It's a surprise," she said, covering up her work with her hands.

Next, she taped the top two **edges** of each sheet of paper together, trying her best to create a cylinder. When she had finished, she disappeared up the stairs with her **treasure**.

It wasn't until later that evening that I noticed a "mailbox" taped onto the doors to each of our bedrooms, there was one for Steve. There was one for Tom. She hadn't forgotten Sam or baby Paul.

For the next few weeks, we received mail on a regular basis. There were little notes confessing her love for each of us. There were short letters full of tiny compliments that only a seven-year-old would notice. I was in charge of retrieving baby Paul's letters, page after page of colored scenes including flowers with happy faces.

"He can't read yet," she **whispered**, "But he can look at the pictures."

Each time I received one of my little girl's gifts, it brightened my heart.

I was touched at how carefully she observed our moods. When Stephen lost a baseball game, there was a letter telling him she thought he was the best ballplayer in the whole world. After I had a particularly hard day, there was a message thanking me for my efforts, complete with a smile face **tucked** near the bottom corner of the page.

This same little girl is grown now, driving off every day to the community college. But some things about her have never changed. One afternoon only a week or so ago, I found a love note next to my bedside.

"Thanks for always being there for me, Mom," it read, "I'm glad that we're the best of friends."

I couldn't help but remember the precious child whose smile has brought me countless hours of joy throughout the years. There are angels among us. I know, I live with one.

霍华德

11 年前，那是一个寒冬的下午。窗外，大片的雪花绕着雪松盘旋飞舞，枝头深绿色的叶尖上挂着小小的冰柱。

我的大儿子史蒂芬去上学了，丈夫里德去上班了，三个小孩挤在橱柜旁，桌面上堆积着蜡笔和记号笔，汤姆正用星星和条纹做徽章，为纸飞机做漂亮的装饰。山姆正忙着自画像，他胖乎乎的小手先画了一个头，然后在本该画身体的位置画了腿和胳膊。孩子们都全神贯注地忙碌着，汤姆不时地告诉弟弟怎样正确地制作一架能够穿行于整间房子的飞机。

我们唯一的女儿劳拉静静地坐在那里，聚精会神地忙着她的事。偶尔她也会问及如何拼写我们家庭某成员的名字，然后极为困难地逐个字母拼写出来。接着，她画了一些有着嫩绿小茎的花朵，在纸张的底部添些草边，每完成一页，她都会在右上角处画一个太阳,周边是蓝天。然后把它们举到眼前欣赏一番,心满意足地长舒一口气。

"宝贝,你干什么呢?"我问道。

看我之前她瞥了一眼她的兄弟们。

"这是一个惊喜。"她双手捂住了作品。

接着,她把每张纸的上下两边粘贴起来,尽量做成一个圆筒。做好后,她带着那些宝贝消失在楼梯上。

直到深夜我才发现,每个人的卧室门上都贴着一个"邮箱"。史蒂夫一个,汤姆一个。她也没把山姆和小保罗忘了。

之后的几周,我们都会定期收到信件。她用这小小的纸条表达了对我们每个人的爱。这些短信满载着一个年仅 7 岁孩子的纯真问候。小保罗的信件由我负责拆阅,那是一页一页的彩色图画,其中有花朵,也有欢乐的笑靥。

"他还不识字,"她喃喃自语道,"但他能看这些图画。"

每次收到小女儿的礼物,我沉闷的心就会豁然开朗。

她对我们心情细微的体察令我颇受感动,史蒂芬输了棒球赛后,便收到了一封信,她认为他是世界上最好的棒球手。如果哪天我特别劳累时,便会收到一封对我的努力表示感谢的信,信纸下角还附有一个笑脸。

如今,那个小女孩已经长大,每天开车上社区学院。但是有些事情她一直都没有改变。大概就在一周前的一个下午,我在床边发现了一张爱的纸条。

"妈妈,感谢您一如既往地支持我,"上面写着,"我为有您这样的好朋友而感到高兴。"

我情不自禁地想起,多年以来,这个可爱孩子的笑容曾带给我无尽的欢乐。人间确有天使,我知道,我正幸运地与其中一位生活在一起。

Practising
& Exercise

实战
提升篇

核心单词

wintry ['wintri] *adj.* 冷淡的；冷漠的
cluster ['klʌstə] *n.* 串，（花等的）束，簇
engross [in'grəus] *v.* 使全神贯注
edge [edʒ] *n.* 边，棱；边缘
treasure ['treʒə] *n.* 财富；贵重物品
whisper ['(h)wispə] *v.* 低语，耳语；私语
tuck [tʌk] *v.* 把……塞进，把……藏入

实用句型

I couldn't help but remember the precious child whose smile has brought me countless hours of joy throughout the years.
我情不自禁地想起，多年以来，这个可爱孩子的笑容曾带给我无尽的欢乐。
① whose 在这里引导定语从句。
② could not help but 禁不住，类似的表达还有 could not help to 不能帮忙做某事等。

翻译行不行

1. 我现在必须集中精力工作。(concentrate on)

....

2. 他们买了一栋家具齐备的房子。(complete with)

....

3. 一位有经验的机械师负责这工作。(in charge of)

....

Visit with a Tramp
一个流浪汉的来访

· Isaac ·

I was swinging on the front gate, trying to decide whether to walk down the street to play with Verna, my best friend in fifth grade, when I saw a tramp come up the road.

"Hello, little girl," he said, "is your mama at home?"

I nodded and swung the gate open to let him in the yard. He looked like all the tramps who came to our house from the hobo camp by the river during the Great Depression. His **shaggy** hair hung below a shapeless hat, and his threadbare shirt and trousers had been rained on and slept in. He smelled like a bonfire.

He shuffled to the door. When my mother **appeared**, he asked, "Lady, could you spare a bite to eat?"

"I think so. Please sit on the step."

He dropped onto the narrow wooden platform that served as the front porch of our two-room frame house. In minutes my mother opened the screen and handed him a sandwich made from thick slices of homemade bread and **generous** chunks of boiled meat. She gave him a tin cup of milk. "I thank you, lady." he said.

I swung on the gate, watching the tramp wolf down the sandwich and drain the cup. Then he stood and walked back through the gate. "They said your mama would feed me." he told me on the way out.

Vema had said the hobos told one another who would feed them. "They never come to my house." she had **announced** proudly.

So why does Mama feed them? I wondered. A widow, she worked as a waitress in the mornings and sewed at night to earn money. Why should she give anything to men who didn't work at all?

I **marched** inside. "Verna's mother says those men are too lazy to work. Why do we feed them?"

My mother smiled. Her blue housedress matched her eyes and emphasized her auburn hair.

"Lovely, we don't know why those men don't work," she said, "but they were babies once. And their mothers loved them, like I love you." *She put her hands on my shoulders and drew me close to her apron*, *which smelled of starch and freshly baked bread.*

"I feed them for their mothers, because if you were ever **hungry** and had nothing to eat, I would want their mothers to feed you."

艾萨克

我在院门口晃悠，想着要不要沿街去找维娜玩，她是我五年级最好的朋友。这时，我看见一个流浪汉从街上走来。

"你好，小姑娘，"他说，"你妈妈在家吗？"

我点点头并把门打开让他进了院子。经济大萧条时期，有许多流浪汉从河那边的游民营来过我家，他看起来跟他们一样。蓬乱的头发从那顶不成型的帽子下露了出来，破破烂烂的衬衣和裤子显然被雨水淋湿过，还穿着睡过觉。他浑身散发着一种篝火烧焦的味道。

他慢吞吞地走到门口。我妈妈出来了，他问，"夫人，能不能给我点吃的？"

"好吧，请坐在台阶上等一下。"

他坐在狭长的木板平台上，那是两间屋的前廊。不一会儿，妈妈打开帘子，递给他一个三明治。用家里自制的厚面包片夹着几大块熟肉。她还给了他一杯牛奶。"谢谢您，夫人。"他说。

我在门口一边晃悠着，一边看着这个流浪汉狼吞虎咽地吃下那个三明治，喝干牛奶。然后，他站起来，穿过了大门往外走。"他们说你妈妈会给我东西吃。"他出门的时候对我说。

维娜曾说过，谁给流浪汉们东西吃，他们就会互相转告。"他们从不去我家。"她骄傲地说道。

妈妈为什么要给他们东西吃呢？我很奇怪。妈妈是一个寡妇，上午在餐厅做服务员，晚上还要做缝纫来挣钱。她为什么要把东西给这些毫不相干的人吃呢？

我大步走进屋子，"维娜的妈妈说，这些人太懒了，都不工作。我们为什么要给他们吃的呢。"

妈妈笑了，她蓝色的围裙和眼睛很相称，也衬托着她赤褐色的头发。

"宝贝，我们不知道他们为什么不工作。"她说，"但他们也曾是孩子，他们的妈妈也爱他们，就像我爱你一样。"她把双手放在我肩头，把我拉到她的身边，围裙散发出浆洗过的和新烤的面包的味道。

"我给他们东西吃，是为了他们的妈妈。如果你饿了，又什么吃的都没有，我希望他们的妈妈也能给你东西吃。"

核心单词

shaggy ['ʃægi] *adj.* 有粗毛的；头发蓬乱的

appear [ə'piə] *v.* 出现；显露

generous ['dʒenərəs] *adj.* 慷慨的，大方的

announce [ə'nauns] *v.* 宣布，发布

march [mɑːtʃ] *n.* 步调，进展

hungry ['hʌŋgri] *adj.* 饥饿的；渴望的

实用句型

She put her hands on my shoulders and drew me close to her apron，which smelled of starch and freshly baked bread.

她把双手放在我肩头，把我拉到她的身边，围裙散发出浆洗过的和新烤的面包的味道。

①这里是由 which 引导的非限定性定语从句。

②put on 穿上，把……放在……上，类似的表达还有 put up 建造；put aside 撇开；put away 把……收起，放好等固定搭配。

翻译行不行

1. 那张沙发当作床用。（serve as）

....

2. 说到德语，我一窍不通。（come to）

....

3. 小男孩还不到上学年龄。（too...to...）

....

Forgotten and Forgiven
忘记并宽容

As i sat perched in the second-floor window of our brick schoolhouse that afternoon, my heart began to sink further with each passing car. This was a day I'd looked forward to for weeks: Miss Pace's fourth-grade, end-of-the-year party. Miss Pace had kept a running countdown on the blackboard all that week, and our class of nine-year-olds had bordered on insurrection by the time the much-anticipated "party Friday" had arrived.

I had happily volunteered my mother when Miss Pace requested cookie volunteers. Mom's chocolate chips reigned supreme on our block, and I knew they'd be a hit with my classmates. But two o'clock passed, and there was no sign of her. Most of the other mothers had already come and gone, dropping off their offerings of punch and crackers, chips, cupcakes and brownies. My mother was missing in action.

"Don't worry, Robbie, she'll be along soon." Miss Pace said as I gazed forlornly down at the street. I looked at the wall clock just in time to see its black minute hand shift to half-past.

Around me, the noisy party raged on, but I wouldn't budge

from my window watch post. Miss Pace did her best to coax me away, but I stayed out, holding out hope that the familiar family car would round the corner, carrying my rightfully embarrassed mother with a tin of her famous cookies tucked under her arm.

The three o'clock bell soon jolted me from my thoughts, and I **dejectedly** grabbed my book bag from my desk and shuffled out the door for home.

On the four-block walk to our house, I plotted my **revenge**. I would slam the front door upon entering, refuse to return her hug when she would rush over to me, and vow never to speak to her again.

The house was empty when I arrived, and I looked for a note on the refrigerator that might explain my mother's absence, but found none. My chin quivered with a mixture of heartbreak and rage. For the first time in my life, my mother had let me down.

I was lying face-down on my bed upstairs when I heard her come through the front door.

"Robbie," she called out a bit urgently, "Where are you?"

I could then hear her darting frantically from room to room, wondering where I could be. I remained silent. In a moment, she mounted the steps—the sounds of her footsteps quickening as she ascended the staircase.

When she entered my room and sat beside me on my bed, I didn't move but instead stared blankly into my pillow refusing to acknowledge her presence.

"I'm so sorry, honey," she said, "I just forgot. I got busy and forgot, plain and simple."

I still didn't move. "Don't forgive her," I told myself, "She humiliated you. She forgot you. Make her pay."

Then my mother did something completely unexpected. She began to laugh. I could feel her shudder as the laughter shook her. It began quietly at first and then increased in its velocity and volume.

I was **incredulous**. How could she laugh at a time like this? I rolled over and faced her, ready to let her see the rage and disappointment in my eyes.

But my mother wasn't laughing at all. She was crying. "I'm so sorry," she sobbed softly, "I let you down. I let my little boy down."

She sank down on the bed and began to weep like a little girl. I was dumbstruck. I had never seen my mother cry. To my understanding, mothers weren't supposed to. I wondered if this was how I looked to her when I cried.

I **desperately** tried to recall her own soothing words from times past when I'd skinned knees or stubbed toes, times when she knew just the right thing to say. But in that moment of tearful plight, words of profundity abandoned me like a worn-out shoe.

"It's okay, Mom," I stammered as I reached out and gently stroked her hair, "We didn't even need those cookies. There was plenty of stuff to eat. Don't cry. It's all right. Really."

My words, as inadequate as they sounded to me, prompted my mother to sit up. She wiped her eyes, and a slight smile began to crease her tear-stained cheeks. I smiled back awkwardly, and she pulled me to her.

We didn't say another word. We just held each other in a long, silent **embrace**. When we came to the point where I would usually pull away, I decided that, this time, I could hold on, perhaps, just a little bit longer.

佚 名

那天下午，我坐在砖石教学楼的二楼的窗台上，心情随着每辆车子驶过而越发低落下去。今天是我盼了几个星期的日子：帕斯小姐的四年级毕业舞会。帕斯小姐从周一就开始在黑板上倒计时，我们这些 9 岁小孩们盼着周五舞会的到来简直等得要造反了。

当帕斯小姐要求家长赞助饼干时，我开心地给我妈妈报了名。妈妈的巧克力饼干在我们小区声名远扬，我知道它们肯定会在我的同学中引起轰动。但是已经两点多了，她的身影还是没有出现。别人的妈妈来，放下她们赞助的饮料、饼干、土豆片、杯仔蛋糕和布朗尼蛋糕（一种巧克力蛋糕），然后走了。可我的妈妈却在活动当时不知去向。

当我孤单单地凝视着街道时，帕斯小姐对我说，"别担心，罗比，她很快就来了。"我看着墙上的钟，正好看到黑色的分针指向半点。

在我周围，喧闹的舞会开始了，但我还是不想离开窗台。帕斯小姐使尽浑身解数想让我从那儿走开，但我还坚守着，期盼着那熟悉的家庭轿车出现在拐角，载着我那理应窘迫不安的妈妈，怀里还有一罐她那著名的饼干。

三点的钟声很快将我从思绪中唤醒。我沮丧地将书包从课桌里拖出，脚步拖沓地走回家去。

走回家要经过四个街区，我琢磨着发脾气的办法。我进门时会将大门狠狠撞上，等她冲过来拥抱我时，不回应她的拥抱，而且再也不和她说话。

等我到家时，家里空无一人。我想从冰箱上找到个能解释妈妈失踪原因的纸条，但什么也没有找到。我又气又恨，下巴都哆嗦了起来。有生以来第一次，我的妈妈让我失望了。

当我听到她从大门进来的声音时，我脸朝下趴在楼上自己的床上。

"罗比，"她喊着，声音中带着些焦急，"你在哪儿？"

我接下来听见她疯了似的从一个房间冲到另一个房间，看我在哪里。我不出声。接下来，是她上楼的声音。她的脚步声越来越快。

当她进到我的房间，坐在床边，我一动也不动，直勾勾地盯着枕头，无视她的存在。

"真抱歉，孩子，"她说道，"我忘了。我一忙起来就忘了，就是这样。"

我仍然一动不动。"不能原谅她，"我告诉自己，"她让你丢脸了。她忘了你。罚她。"

接下来我妈妈做了一件完全出乎我意料的事。她笑了。我能感觉到她的身子在颤抖，起初她的笑是无声的，渐渐地动作幅度越来越大。

我疑惑了。这个时候她怎么笑得出来？我转过来看着她，让她看清楚我眼中的怒气和失望。

可是妈妈并不是在笑。她是在哭。"真对不起，"她轻轻地啜泣着，"我让你失望了，我让我的小宝贝失望了。"

她伏在床上，像个孩子似的哭了起来。我被吓呆了。我从来没见过妈妈哭。在我的概念里，妈妈都是不哭的人。我不知道当我哭的时候，她是不是也是这么想的。

我拼命回想过去当我蹭破了膝盖或撞伤了脚趾时她对我说过的那些抚慰的话，那些时候她总是会说出最恰当的话。但是面对这个泪水涟涟的场面，那些深邃的话语，就像丢掉的一双旧鞋那样弃我而去了。

"没关系，妈妈，"我边支支吾吾地说，边伸手轻抚她的头发，"我们其实不需要那些饼干。有好多好多吃的。别哭了。没关系，真的。"

我的话让自己听上去是那么干巴巴，却让我的妈妈坐了起来。她擦擦眼睛，一抹微笑从她泪痕斑斑的脸上浮现。我也傻傻地冲她笑着，她一把将我拉到了怀里。

我们没有再说一句话。我们只是静静地拥抱着。当到了按惯例我会松开的时候，我决定，这次，我可以就这样，也许，再久一点点。

核心单词

reign [rein] *n.* 统治；支配

forlornly [fə'lɔ:nli] *adv.* 可怜地；孤苦伶仃地

dejectedly [di'dʒektidli] *adv.* 沮丧地，灰心地

revenge [ri'vendʒ] *v.* 替……报仇；报复，

incredulous [əin'kredjuləs] *adj.* 不相信的；怀疑的

desperately ['despəritli] *adv.* 绝望地；拼命地

embrace [im'breis] *v.* 拥抱；包括，包含

实用句型

I could then hear her darting frantically from room to room, wondering where I could be. 我接下来听见她疯了似的从一个房间冲到另一个房间，不知道我去了哪里。

①现在分词 wondering 在句中作状语。

②frantically 狂暴地，疯狂似地，是由 frantic 加表方式，程度的副词后缀 ally 构成的。类似的词还有 conditionally 有条件地；systematically 有系统地等。

翻译行不行

1. 我们期待着她的来访。(look forward to)

....

2. 开始我们用手工工具，后来才有了机器。(at first)

....

3. 这些新法令本应该起到防止犯罪的作用。(be supposed to)

....

A Letter to My Son
一封给我儿子的信

• Jason •

Dear Seth,

You're only three years old, and at this point in your life you can't read, much less understand what I'm going to try to tell you in this letter. But I've been thinking a lot about the life that you have **ahead** of you, about my life so far as I reflect on what I've learned, and about my role as a dad in trying to prepare you for the **trials** that you will face in the coming years.

You won't be able to understand this letter today, but someday, when you're ready, I hope you will find some wisdom and value in what I share with you.

You are young, and life has yet to take its toll on you, to throw disappointments and heartaches and loneliness and struggles and pain into your path. You have not been worn down yet by long hours of thankless work, by the slings and **arrows** of everyday life.

For this, be thankful. You are at a wonderful stage of life. You have many wonderful stages of life still to come, but they are not without their costs and **perils**.

I hope to help you along your path by sharing some of the

best of what I've learned. As with any advice, take it with a grain of salt. What works for me might not work for you.

Life Can Be Cruel

There will be people in your life who won't be very nice. They'll tease you because you're different, or for no good reason. They might try to **bully** you or hurt you.

There's not much you can do about these people except to learn to deal with them, and learn to choose friends who are kind to you, who **actually** care about you, who make you feel good about yourself. When you find friends like this, hold on to them, treasure them, spend time with them, be kind to them, love them.

There will be times when you are met with disappointment instead of success. Life won't always turn out the way you want. *This is just another thing you'll have to learn to deal with*. But instead of letting these things get you down, push on. Accept disappointment and learn to persevere, to pursue your dreams despite pitfalls. Learn to turn **negatives** into positives, and you'll do much better in life.

You will also face heartbreak and abandonment by those you love. I hope you don't have to face this too much, but it happens. Again, not much you can do but to heal, and to move on with your life. Let these pains become stepping stones to better things in life, and learn to use them to make you stronger.

But Be Open to life Anyway

Yes, you'll find cruelty and suffering in your journey through life...but don't let that close you to new things. Don't retreat from life, don't hide or wall yourself off. Be open to new things, new experiences, new people.

You might get your heart broken 10 times, but find the most

wonderful woman the 11th time. If you shut yourself off from love, you'll miss out on that woman, and the happiest times of your life.

You might get teased and bullied and hurt by people you meet...and then after meeting dozens of jerks, find a true friend. If you close yourself off to new people, and don't open your heart to them, you'll avoid pain...but also lose out on meeting some **incredible** people, who will be there during the toughest times of your life and create some of the best times of your life.

You will fail many times but if you allow that to stop you from trying, you will miss out on the amazing feeling of success once you reach new heights with your accomplishments. Failure is a stepping stone to success.

Life Isn't a Competition

You will meet many people who will try to outdo you, in school, in college, at work. They'll try to have nicer cars, bigger houses, nicer clothes, cooler gadgets. To them, life is a competition—they have to do better than their peers to be happy.

Here's a secret: Life isn't a competition. It's a journey. If you spend that journey always trying to impress others, to outdo others, you're wasting your journey. Instead, learn to enjoy the journey. Make it a journey of happiness, of constant learning, of continual improvement, of love.

Don't worry about having a nicer car or house or anything material, or even a better-paying job. None of that matters a whit, and none of it will make you happier. You'll acquire these things and then only want more. Instead, learn to be satisfied with having enough—and then use the time you would have wasted trying to earn money to buy those things... use that time doing things you love.

Find your passion, and pursue it doggedly. Don't settle for a job that pays the bills. Life is too short to waste on a job you hate.

Love Should Be Your Rule

If there's a single word you should live your life by, it should be this: Love. It might sound corny, I know...but trust me, there's no better rule in life.

Some would live by the rule of success. Their lives will be stressful, unhappy and shallow.

Others would live by the rule of selfishness—putting their needs above those of others. They will live lonely lives, and will also be unhappy.

Still others will live by the rule of righteousness—trying to show the right path, and admonishing anyone who doesn't live by that path. They are concerned with others, but in a negative way, and in the end will only have their own righteousness to live with, and that's a horrible companion.

Live your life by the rule of love. Love your spouse, your children, your parents, your friends, with all of your heart. Give to them what they need, and show them not cruelty nor disapproval nor coldness nor disappointment, but only love. Open your soul to them.

Love not only your loved ones, but your neighbors... your coworkers... strangers... your brothers and sisters in humanity. Offer anyone you meet a smile, a kind word, a kind gesture, a helping hand.

Love not only neighbors and strangers...but your enemy. The person who is cruelest to you, who has been unkind to you... love him. He is a tortured soul, and most in need of your love.

And most of all, love yourself. While others may criticize you, learn not to be so hard on yourself, to think that you're ugly or dumb or unworthy of love...but to think instead that you are a wonderful human being, worthy of happiness and love... and learn to love yourself for who you are.

Finally, know that I love you and always will. You are starting out on a weird, scary, daunting, but ultimately incredibly wonderful journey, and I will be there for you when I can. Godspeed.

Love, Your Dad

詹　森

亲爱的 Seth：

你现在只有三岁，还无法阅读，更无法理解在这封信里我想要告诉你的。我想了很多，有关于你未来所要面对的生活，有到目前为止我在生活中所学会的东西，和作为一个父亲我将尽可能为你未来所要面对的考验做的准备。

你现在还不能理解这封信，但是有一天，当你准备好了，我希望你能在这里找到我要与你分享的智慧和价值。

你现在还小，还没有感受到生命的代价，生活中会有失望、烦恼、孤独挣扎和伤痛。你还没有因为长时间无回报的工作和日常生活中的荆棘而一蹶不振。

对于这一点，我感到很庆幸。你现在正处在一个很美好的生活阶段。在你的生活中将有很多精彩的阶段，但它们同样伴随着代价和危险。

我希望能把我在人生中学到的最好的东西与你分享。对于任何建议，都应当稍加分析。那些对我有用的东西不一定适合你。

生活可能很残酷

你生活中遇到的某些人可能不是很友善。可能因为你的与众不同，或者没有任何理由，他们会嘲笑你。他们可能会欺辱你或者伤害你。

对于这些人你除了学会要对付他们之外，没有什么可做的，并且要学会选择那些对你友善，真正关心你并且让你感觉良好的人做朋友。当你找到这种朋友时，就要把握住他们，珍惜他们，与他们共处，对他们友善，并且要爱他们。

将来有时候你可能会遭遇失败而非成功。生活不可能总按你希望的方向发展。这是另一件你必须学会处理的事情。你应当推动事情向你所希望的方向发展，而不是任它摆布。接受失望并且学会坚持，即使遭遇困难也要追求梦想。学会把消极的转化为积极的，这样你就能在生活中表现得更好。

你也会遭到爱人的抛弃。我希望你不要太多的面对这些，但是这确实会发生。同样，你也只能慢慢治愈，并且继续你的生活。让这些伤害变成你追求更好生活的踏脚石，并且要利用它们使你自己变得更强。

要乐意接受生活中的方方面面

你将会在人生的旅途中遭遇到残忍和不幸……但是不要让那些束缚你去接触新的事物。不要远离生活，不要隐藏或隔离自己。让自己去接触一些新的事物，新的经验和新的朋友。

你也许会伤心十次，但是却在第十一次找到了最棒的女人。如果你封闭自己不去爱的话，你就会失去那个女人和你生命中最快乐的时光。

　　你也许会被你遇到的人嘲笑和欺侮……但是当你遇到一群蠢人的时候，你随后就会找到真正的朋友。如果你封闭自己不去接触一些不认识的人，不和他们以诚相待的话，你会避免受到伤害……同时，你也会错过一些难以置信的人，这些人将会陪你度过生命中最艰难的时光和为你创造生命中最辉煌的日子。

　　你也许会失败很多次，但是如果你让那些失败阻止你去进行新的尝试的话，一旦你的成就到达新的高度时，你将失去那种成功的美妙感觉。失败乃成功之母。

生活不是一场竞赛

　　你会碰到很多人，他们会在中学、大学以及工作中试着要超过你。他们想拥有更好的车，更大的房子，更漂亮的衣服，更酷的设备。对他们来说，生活就是一场竞赛——他们只有比同龄人更强他们才会感到快乐。

　　这里有一个秘密：生活不是一场竞赛。它是一个旅程。如果你在旅程中只是花时间让别人佩服你和超过别人，那么你就是在浪费你的旅程。相反，你应该学会享受旅程。把它当作一次快乐的、不断学习的、不断进步的和爱的旅程。

　　不要为拥有更好的汽车、房子或者其他物质的条件，甚至是一份高薪的工作而烦恼。它们一点都不值得，且它们也没法让你变得更快乐。当你获得这些东西以后你会想得到更多。相反，你要学会满足于自己所拥有的东西——然后用你原本准备赚钱买那些东西的时间……用那些时间去做一些你喜欢的事情吧。

　　寻找你的兴趣，并且持之以恒地追求它。不要为了一份高薪而去工作。生命太短暂了，不要将其浪费在自己不喜欢的工作上。

爱应该是你生活中的法则

　　如果用一个词来形容你应该如何生活的话，那么它应该是：爱。我知道，它也许听起来很老套……但是相信我，生活中没有更好的规则了。

有些人也许会把成功当作生活中的准则。他们的生活将会是压力重重，不快乐的而且是肤浅的。

其他人也许会以自私为准则——把他们自身的需要凌驾于其他人之上。他们的生活会很孤单，而且也不会快乐。

同样还要一些人以公正为准则——试图为其他人引领正确的道路，并且会警告那些没有按照他的道路生活的人们。他们总在关注着别人，但是却以一种消极的方式，最后他们只能在生活中与公正为伍，这是一个可怕的同伴。

你的生活应该以爱为准则。全身心地去爱你的伴侣，你的孩子，你的父母，你的朋友。给予他们所需要的，并且给予他们的不是残酷，不是反对，不是失望，而只是爱。把你的心向他们敞开。

不仅仅只爱你所爱的人，要以仁爱的心去爱你的邻居，你的工作伙伴，陌生人以及你的同胞。给你所遇见的人一个微笑，一句友善的话，一个友好的手势，以及帮助。

不仅要爱你的邻居、陌生人，也要爱你的敌人。那个对你最残酷，对你不友好的人，也请你去爱他。他的灵魂是扭曲的，所以他最需要你的爱。

最重要的是要爱你自己。当其他人批评你的时候，学会不要苛刻地对待自己，不要认为自己很丑或很蠢甚至不值得被爱……而要认为自己是一个不错的人，值得拥有快乐和爱……并且要学会为了自己去爱自己。

最后，你要知道我爱你并且永远都会深爱着你。你将要开始一个无法预测的、可怕的、令人畏缩的，但最终却非常美好的旅程，我将会尽我最大可能陪在你身边。祝你一路平安。

爱你的爸爸

核心单词

ahead [ə'hed] *adv.* 在前；向前

trial ['traiəl] *n.* 试用；试验；考验

arrow ['ærəu] *n.* 箭；箭状物

peril ['peril] *n.* 危险

bully ['buli] *n.* 恶霸 *v.* 威吓，胁迫

actually ['æktʃuəli] *adv.* 实际上，真的

negative ['negətiv] *adj.* 否定的；消极的

incredible [in'kredəbl] *adj.* 不可信的；惊人的；极妙的

实用句型

This is just another thing you'll have to learn to deal with.

这是另一件你必须学会处理的事情。

①这是一句省略了引导词 that 的定语从句。

②have to 和 must 都表"必须"，区别是 have to 表客观的需要，而 must 表说话人主观上的看法，既主观上的必要。

翻译行不行

1. 他已学会恰当地应付各种复杂局面了。(deal with)

....

2. 他们出门前要把家中的煤气和电源都关掉。(shut off)

....

3. 像他这样的人永远不满足于现状。(be satisfied with)

....

The Apple Tree
苹果树

A long time ago, there was a huge apple tree. A little boy loved to come and lay around it every day. He climbed to the tree top, ate the apples, took a nap under the shadow... He loved the tree and the tree loved to play with him.

Time went by... the little boy had grown up and he no longer played around the tree every day. One day, the boy came back to the tree and he looked sad "Come and play with me," the tree asked the boy. "I am no longer a kid, I don't play around trees anymore." The boy replied, "I want toys. I need money to buy them." "Sorry, but I don't have money...but you can pick all my apples and sell them. So, you will have money." The boy was so excited. He **grabbed** all the apples on the tree and left happily. The boy never came back after he picked the apples. The tree was sad.

One day, the boy returned and the tree was so excited. "Come and play with me," the tree said. "I don't have time to play. I have to work for my family. We need a house for **shelter**. Can you help me?" "Sorry, but I don't have a house. But you can chop off my **branches** to build your house." So the boy cut all the branches off the tree and left happily. The tree was glad to see him happy but the boy never came back since then. The tree was again lonely and sad.

One hot summer day, the boy returned and the tree was **delighted**. "Come and play with me!" the tree said. "I am sad and getting old. I want to go sailing to relax myself. Can you give me a boat?" "Use my trunk to build your boat. You can sail far away and be happy." So the boy cut the tree trunk to make a boat. He went sailing and never showed up for a long time. The tree was happy, but it was not true.

Finally, the boy returned after he left for so many years. "Sorry, my boy. But I don't have anything for you anymore. No more apples for you..." the tree said.

"I don't have teeth to bite," the boy replied.

"No more trunk for you to climb on."

"I am too old for that now," the boy said.

"I really can't give you anything... the only thing left is my **dying** roots," the tree said with tears.

"I don't need much now, just a place to rest. I am tired after all these years." The boy replied.

"Good! Old tree roots are the best place to lean on and rest. Come, Come sit down with me and rest." The boy sat down and the tree was glad and smiled with tears...

This is a story of everyone. The tree is our parent. When we were young, we loved to play with Mom and Dad... When we grown up, we left them, and only came to them when we need something or when we are in trouble. No matter what, parents will always be there and give everything they could to make you happy. You may think that the boy is **cruel** to the tree but that's how all of us are treating our parents.

杰罗姆

　　很久很久以前，有一棵又高又大的苹果树。一个小男孩，天天到树下来玩，他爬上去摘苹果吃，在树阴下睡觉。他爱苹果树，苹果树也爱和他一起玩。

　　后来，小男孩长大了，不再天天来玩了。一天他又来到树下，很伤心的样子。苹果树说："和我一起玩吧。"男孩说："不行，我不小了，不能再和你玩了，我想要玩具，可是没钱买。"苹果树说："很遗憾，我也没钱，不过，把我所有的果子摘下来卖掉，你不就有钱了吗？"男孩十分激动。他摘了所有的苹果，高高兴兴地走了。然后，男孩好久都没有来。苹果树很伤心。

　　有一天，男孩终于来了，树很是兴奋，说："和我一起玩吧。"男孩说："不行，我没有时间，我要为家而奋斗，我们需要一幢房子，你能帮我吗？""对不起，我没有房子，"苹果树说，"不过你可以用我的树枝去搭房子。"于是，男孩砍下所有的树枝，高高兴兴地运去盖房子了。看到男孩高兴，树好快乐。从此，男孩又不来了。树再次陷入了孤单和悲伤之中。

　　一个炎热的夏天，男孩回来了，树太高兴了："来呀！孩子，来和我玩呀。"男孩却说："我心情不好，一天天老了，我想扬帆出海，去轻松一下，你能给我一艘船吗？"苹果树说："把我的树干砍去，拿去做船吧！"于是男孩砍下了它的树干，造了条船，然后高兴地驾船走了。树看到男孩高兴它也很高兴，但男孩又是很久没有回来。树再次陷入了孤单和悲伤之中。

许多年过去了，男孩终于回来了。苹果树说："对不起，孩子，我已经没有东西可以给你了，我没有苹果了。"

男孩说："我的牙都掉了，吃不了苹果了。"

苹果树又说："我没有可以让你爬的树干了。"

男孩说："我老了，爬不动了。"

"我再也没有什么能给你的了……，只剩下这枯死的老根了，"树老泪纵横地说。

男孩说："这么多年过去了，现在我感到累了，什么也不想要了，只要一个休息的地方。"

"好啊！老根是最适合坐下来休息的，来啊，坐下来和我一起休息吧！"男孩坐下来了，苹果树高兴得流下了热泪……

这就是我们每个人的故事。这棵树就是我们的父母。小时候，我们喜欢和爸爸妈妈玩……长大后，我们就离开了他们，只有在需要什么东西或遇到麻烦的时候，才会回到他们的身边。无论如何，父母永远都在那儿，倾其所有使你快乐。你可能认为这个男孩对树很残酷，但这就是我们每个人对待父母的方式。

核心单词

grab [græb] *v.* 攫取，抓取

shelter ['ʃeltə] *n.* 遮盖物；躲避处

branch [brɑːntʃ] *n.* 树枝；支线；支路

delighted [di'laitid] *adj.* 高兴的，快乐的

dying ['daiiŋ] *adj.* 垂死的；快熄灭的

cruel ['kruəl] *adj.* 残忍的，残酷的

实用句型

Time went by... the little boy had grown up and he no longer played around the tree every day.

后来，小男孩长大了，不再天天来玩耍了。

①had grown 是过去完成时 had+done 的形式。

②no longer 不再，等于 not...any longer。

翻译行不行

1. 小男孩正在玩一架玩具飞机。(play with)

....

2. 我明天动身去伦敦。(leave for)

....

3. 他总是依赖别人的帮助。(lean on)

....

我希望有人在什么地方**等我**

I wish someone were waiting for me somewhere

The Love Letter
迟到的情书

• Melissa Nevels •

I was always a little in awe of great-aunt Stephina Roos. *Indeed, as children we were all frankly terrified of her*. The fact that she did not live with the family, preferring her tiny cottage and **solitude** to the comfortable but rather noisy household where we were brought up— added to the respectful fear in which she was held.

We used to take it in turn to carry small delicacies which my mother had made down from the big house to the little cottage where Aunt Stephia and an old colored maid spent their days. Old Tnate Sanna would open the door to the rather frightened little messenger and would usher him or her into the dark voor-kamer, where the shutters were always closed to keep out the heat and the flies. There we would wait, in trembling but not altogether unpleasant.

She was a tiny little woman to inspire so much **veneration**. She was always dressed in black, and her dark clothes melted into the shadows of the voor-kamer and made her look smaller than ever. But you felt, the moment she entered, that something vital and strong and somehow indestructible had come in with her, although she moved slowly, and her voice was sweet and soft.

She never embraced us. She would greet us and take out hot little hands in her own beautiful cool one, with blue veins standing out on the back of it, as though the white skin were almost too

delicate to contain them.

Tnate Sanna would bring in dishes of sweet, sweet, sticky candy, or a great bowl of grapes or peaches, and great-aunt Stephina would converse gravely about happenings on the farm, and, more rarely, of the outer world.

When we had finished our sweetmeats or fruit she would accompany us to the stoep, bidding us thank our mother for her gift and sending quaint, old-fashioned messages to her and father. Then she would turn and enter the house, closing the door behind, so that it became once more a place of **mystery**.

As I grew older I found, rather to my surprise, that I had become genuinely fond of my aloof old great-aunt. But to this day I do not know what strange impulse made me take George to see her and to tell her, before I had confided in another living soul, of our engagement. To my astonishment, she was delighted.

"An Englishman" she exclaimed. "But that is splendid, splendid. And you," she turned to George" you are making your home in this country? You do not intend to return to England just yet?

She seemed relieved when she heard that George had bought a farm near our own farm and intended to settle in South Africa. She became quite animated, and chattered away to him.

After that I would often slip away to the little cottage by the mealie Lands. Once she was somewhat disappointed on hearing that we had decided to wait for two years before getting married, but when she learned that my father and mother were both pleased with the match she seemed reassured.

Still, she often appeared **anxious** ahout my love affair, and would ask questions that seemed to me strange, almost as though she feared that something would happen to destroy my romance. But I was quite unprepared for her outburst when

I mentioned that George thought of paying a lightning visit to England before we were married. "He must not do it'" she cried. "Ina, you must not let him go. Promise me you will prevent him." she was trembling all over. I did what I could to console her, but she looked so tired and pale that I persuaded her to go to her room and rest, promising to return the next day.

When I arrived I found her sitting on the step. She looked lonely and **pathetic**, and for the first time I wondered why no man had ever taken her and looked after her and loved her. Mother had told me that great-aunt Stephina had been lovely as a young girl, and although no trace of that beauty remained, except perhaps in her brown eyes, yet she looked so small and appealing that any man, one felt, would have wanted to protect her. She paused, as though she did not quite know how to begin. Then she seemed to give herself, mentally, a litile shake. "You must have wondered", she said, "why I was so upset at the thought of young George's going to England without you. I am an old woman, and perhaps I have the silly fancies of the old, but I should like to tell you my own love story, and then you can decide whether it is wise for your man to leave you before you are married."

"I was quite a young girl when I first met Richard Weston. He was an Englishman who boarded with the Van Rensburgs on the next farm, four or five miles from us. Richard was not strong. He had a weak chest, and the doctors had sent him to South Africa so that the dry air could cure him. He taught the Van Rensburg children, who were younger than I was, though we often played together, but he did this for pleasure and not because he needed money.

"We loved one another from the first moment we met, though we did not speak of our love until the evening of my eighteenth birthday. All our friends and relatives had come to my party, and in the evening we danced on the big old carpet which we had laid down in the barn. Richard had come with the Van Rensburgs, and we danced together as often as we dared, which was not very often, for my father hated the Uitlanders. Indeed, for a time he had quarreled with Mynheer Van Rensburg for allowing Richard to board with him, but aferwards he got used to the idea, and was always polite to the Englishman, though he never liked him.

"That was the happiest birthday of my life, for while we were resting between dances Richard took me outside into the cool, moonlit night, and there, under the stars' he told me he loved me and asked me to marry him. Of course I promised I would, for I was too happy to think of what my parents would say, Or indeed of anything except Richard was not at our meeting place as he had arranged. I was disappointed but not alarmed, for so many things could happen to either of us to prevent out keeping our tryst. I thought that next time we visited the Van Ransburgs, I should hear what had kept him and we could plan further meetings...

"So when my father asked if I would drive with him to Driefontein I was delighted. But when we reached the homestead and were sitting on the step drinking our coffee, we heard that Richard had left quite suddenly and had gone back to England. His father had died, and now he was the heir and must go back to look after his estates.

"I do not remember very much more about that day, except that the sun seemed to have stopped shining and the country no longer looked beautiful and full of promise, but bleak and **desolate** as it sometimes does in winter or in times of drought. Late that afternoon, Jantje, the Little Hottentot herd boy, came up to me and handed me a letter, which he said the English baas had left for me. It was the only love letter I ever received, but it turned all my bitterness and grief into a peacefulness which was the nearest I could get, then, to happiness. I knew Richard still loved me, and somehow, as long as I had his letter, I felt that we could never be really parted, even if he were in England and I had to remain on the farm. I have it yet, and though I am an old, tired woman, it still gives me hope and courage.

"It must have heen a wonderful letter, Aunt Stephia," I said.

The old lady came back from her dreams of that far-off romance. "Perhaps," she said, hesitating a little, "perhaps, my dear, you would care to read it ?"

"I should love to, Aunt Stephia," I said gently.

She rose at once and tripped into the house as eagerly as a young girl. When she came back she handed me a letter, **faded** and yellow with age, the edges of the envelope worn and frayed as though it had been much handled. But when I came to open it I found that the seal was unbroken.

"Open it, open it'" said great-aunt Stephia, and her voice was shaking.

I broke the seal and read.

It was not a love letter in the true sense of the word, but pages of the minutest directions of how "my sweetest Phina" was to **elude** her father's vigilance, creep down to the drift at night and there meet Jantje with a horse which would take her to Smitsdorp. There she was to go to "my true friend, Henry Wilson", who would give her money and make arrangements for her to follow her lover to Cape Town and from there to England, "where, my love, we can be married at once. But if, my dearest, you are not sure that you can face life with me in a land strange to you, then do not take this important step, for I love you too much to wish you the smallest unhappiness. If you do not come, and if I do not hear from you, then I shall know that you could never be happy so far from the people and the country which you love. If, however, you feel you can keep your promise to me, but are of too timid and modest a journey to England unaccompanied, then write to me, and I will, by some means, return to fetch my bride."

I read no further.

"But Aunt Phina!" I gasped. "Why... why... ?"

The old lady was watching me with trembling eagerness, her face flushed and her eyes bright with expectation. "Read it aloud, my dear," she said. "I want to hear every word of it. There was never anyone I could trust... Uitlanders were hated in my young days... I could not ask anyone."

"But, Auntie, don't you even know what he wrote?"

The old lady looked down, troubled and shy like a child who has **unwittingly** done wrong.

"No, dear," she said, speaking very low. "You see, I never learned to read."

梅丽莎·内维尔斯

我对斯蒂菲娜姑姑总是怀着敬畏之情。说实话，我们几个孩子对她都怕得要死。她宁愿住在她的小屋子里，也而不愿住在舒舒服服、热热闹闹的家里——我们6个孩子都是在家里长大的——这更加重了我们对她的敬畏之情。

我们经常轮流带着母亲做的可口食品到她和一名黑人女仆

一起生活的那间小屋去。桑娜阿姨总是为每一个怯生生的小使者打开房门，将他或她领进昏暗的客厅。那里的百叶窗长年都关闭着，以防热气和苍蝇进去。我们总是在那里哆哆嗦嗦的，但也不是完全不高兴地等着斯蒂菲娜姑姑出来。

像她那样身材纤细的女人居然能赢得我们如此的尊敬。她总是身穿黑色衣服，与客厅里的阴暗背景融为一体，这将她的身材衬托得更加娇小。但她一进门，我们就感到有一种说不清道不明、充满活力和刚强的气氛，尽管她脚步缓慢、声调甜柔。

她从不拥抱我们，但总是和我们寒暄，用她那双秀美清爽的手握着我们热乎乎的小手。她的手背上暴露出一些青筋，感觉手上的皮肤白嫩细薄得遮不住它们似的。

桑娜阿姨每次都要端出几碟黏糊糊的南非糖果和一钵葡萄或桃子给我们吃。斯蒂菲娜姑姑总是一本正经地说些农场里的事，偶尔也谈些世界上的事。

等我们吃完糖果或水果，她总要将我们送到屋前的门廊，叮嘱我们要多谢母亲给她送食品，要我们对父母亲转达一些稀奇古怪的老式祝愿，然后就转身回到屋里，随手关上门，那里再次成了神秘世界。

随着年龄的增长，我惊奇地发现，我打心眼里喜欢起我那位孤零零的老姑姑来。至今我仍不知道那是一种什么样的奇异动力，使我在没有向别人透露之前就带着乔治去看望姑姑，告诉她我们已经订婚的消息。不曾想，听到这个消息以后，她竟非常高兴。

"是英国人！"她惊讶地大声说道，"好极了。你，"她转向乔治，"你要在南非安家吗？你现在不打算回国吧？"

当听说乔治已经在我们农场附近购置了一片农场并打算定居下来时，她好像松了一口气。她兴致勃勃地和乔治攀谈起来。

从那以后，我经常到那个位于玉米地边的小屋。有一次，当斯蒂菲娜姑姑听说我们决定再过两年结婚时，露出了失望的神色。但当听说我的父母亲都同意这门亲事时，她又放宽了心。

但她对我的婚姻大事还是经常挂在嘴边。她常常问一些怪怪的问题，似乎担心我的婚事会告吹一样。当我提到乔治打算在婚前回国一段时间时，她竟激动了起来。只见她浑身哆嗦着大声嚷道："他不能回去！爱娜！你不能放他走，你得答应我不放他走！"我尽力安慰她，但她还是显得萎靡不振。我只好劝她回屋休息，并答应第二天再去看她。

我第二天去看她时，她正坐在屋前的台阶上，流露出抑郁的神情。我第一次感到纳闷：以前怎么没有人娶她，没人照料和爱抚她呢？记得母亲曾经说过，斯蒂菲娜姑姑以前是一个可爱的小姑娘。除了她那褐色的眼睛尚能保留一点昔日的风韵之外，她的美貌早已荡然无存，但她看上去还是那样小巧玲珑，惹人怜爱，能引起男人的惜香怜玉之情。她看着我欲言又止，好像不知道从何说起似的。接着，她仿佛振作了起来。她说："我听你说乔治要回国，又不带你走，心里非常不安。我这份心事你是不明白的。我是一个老婆子了，大概还怀着老人们的那颗痴心吧。不过，我想把自己的爱情故事讲给你听。这样你就能明白在你们结婚之前让你的未婚夫离开，不是一个明智之举。

"我第一次遇见理查德·威斯顿时还很年轻。他是一个英国人，寄宿在离我家四五英里的一个农场上的范·伦斯堡家里。他身体不好，胸闷气短。医生让他去南非，因为干燥的气候对他的病有好处。他教伦斯堡的孩子们念书，他们都比我小，可我们还是经常在一块玩。理查德是以教书为乐，并不是为了赚钱。

"我和理查德一见钟情，尽管直到我 18 岁生日那天我们才表达彼此的爱慕之情。我的亲友都参加了那晚的舞会。我们在仓房里铺的一条宽大的旧毛毯上翩翩起舞。理查德是和范·伦斯堡一起来的，我和他壮着胆子频频起舞，但事实上并没有几次，因为我的父亲很讨厌'洋人'。有一次，他曾抱怨说伦斯堡先生不应该让理查德寄住在他的家里，为此还跟他吵过一架，可后来就习以为常了。虽谈不上喜欢，但他对这个英国人还是以礼相待。

"那是我一生中过得最快乐的一个生日，因为理查德在舞会上将我领到外面，在清凉的月光下，在点点繁星下对我倾诉爱慕之情，并向我求婚。我二话没说就答应了，因为我早已心醉神迷，根本顾不上考虑父母的态度。我的心中除了理查德和他的爱情，什么也顾不上了。

直到后来的一天，在他安排的约会处，理查德爽约没有来。失望之际，我没有大惊小怪，因为谁都会碰到形形色色的事而无法赴会。我想去范·伦斯堡家看看就会知道理查德未能赴约的原因，然后再安排接下来的约会……

"所以，当父亲问我是否愿意和他一块去德里方丹时，我就高兴地答应了。但等我们赶到范·伦斯堡家，坐在他们家屋前的门廊上喝咖啡时，却听说理查德已经不辞而别回英国去了。他的父亲死了，他作为继承人，不得不回去料理遗产。

"那天的事我记不大清楚了，只记得当时阳光惨淡，田野也失去了美丽的风采和欣欣向荣的景象，萧瑟凄凉得跟冬天或大旱时一样。那天傍晚，在我和父亲动身回家之前，小牧童詹杰交给找一封信，他说是那位英国老爷留给我的。这可是我有生以来收到的唯一的情书！它将我的忧伤一扫而光，使我的心情变得平静——当时对我来说几乎是类似幸福的平静。我知道理查德仍爱着我。不知怎么回事，有了这封信，我便觉得我们不可能真正分开，哪怕是他在英国，我在南非的农场。这封信我至今仍保留着，尽管我已经年迈体衰，但它仍能带给我希望和勇气。"

"斯蒂菲娜姑姑，那封信一定美极了吧？"我说。

老太太从她那久远的爱之梦中醒过神来。"也许，"她带着犹豫的神情说，"也许，亲爱的，你想看看那封信吧？"

"我很想看，斯蒂菲娜姑姑。"我轻声说。

她猛地站起身，奔进屋里，急切得像个小姑娘。她从屋里出来，递给我一封信。由于时日已久，信纸已经褪色发黄，信封边也有所磨损，好像曾被摩挲过好多次。但当我取信时，我发现封口还没有拆开。

"拆开，拆开吧！"斯蒂菲娜老姑声音颤抖地说。

我撕开封口，开始念信。

严格地说，这算不上是情书，实际上只是几页内容详尽的行动指南。信里告诉"我最亲爱的菲娜"该怎么摆脱她父亲的监视，夜里逃出家门，詹杰会在浅滩上牵马等着她，然后将她驮到史密斯多普，到了那里再去找理查德的"知心朋友亨利·威尔逊"，他会给她钱并为她安排跟随她的情人到开普敦，随后转道英国。"亲爱的，这样我们就可以在英国结婚了。但是我的至爱，如果你不能保证你能在一个陌生的地方和我一块生活，你就不要采取这个重大行动了，因为我太爱你了，不想让你有丝毫不快。如果你不来，如果我没有收到你的回信，我就会知道，如果你离开你挚爱的亲人和乡土，你是不会幸福的。但如果你能实践你对我的许诺而由于你生性持重不愿只身前往英国，就来信告诉我，那我就会设法回南非来迎娶我的新娘。"

我没有再念下去。

"可是，菲娜姑姑，"我急切地说，"为什么……？为什么……？"

老太太的身子由于渴望知道信的内容而颤抖，她注视着我，脸庞因急切的期待而一片绯红。"亲爱的，大声念吧！"她说，"信里的一字一句，我都要听！当时我找不到可靠的人给我念……我年轻时，'洋人'是被人深恶痛绝的……我找不到人给我念啊！"

"可是姑姑，难道你一直不知道信的内容吗？"

老太太低着头，像一个无心做错事的怯生生的孩子。

"不知道，亲爱的，"她低声说，"你知道，我从来没有念过书啊！"

Practising & Exercise 实战提升篇

核心单词

solitude ['sɔlitjuːd] *n.* 孤独；寂寞

veneration [,venə'reiʃən] *n.* 尊敬

delicate ['delikit] *adj.* 精美的，雅致的

mystery ['mistəri] *n.* 神秘，秘密

anxious ['æŋkʃəs] *adj.* 焦虑的，挂念的

pathetic [pə'θetik] *adj.* 引起怜悯的；可怜的；可悲的

desolate ['desəlit] *adj.* 荒芜的，无人烟

fade [feid] *v.* 凋谢，枯萎

elude [əi'ljuːd] *v.* (巧妙地) 逃避，躲避

unwittingly [,ʌn'witiŋli] *adv.* 无意地；不经意地

实用句型

Indeed, as children we were all frankly tenified of her.

说实话，我们几个孩子对她都怕得要死。

① as 在这里做介词。

② frankly 真诚地，类似的 ady+ly 构成 adv 的有：rapid → rapidly；careful → carefully 等。

翻译行不行

1. 许多男孩的梦想是成为飞行员。(dream of)

....

2. 马上就做！(at once)

....

3. 我累得都动不了了。(too...to)

....

A Walk in The Woods
林中漫步

• Justin •

I was **puzzled**! *Why was this old woman making such a fuss about an old copse which was of no use to anybody?* She had written letters to the local paper, even to a national, **protesting** about a projected by-pass to her village, and, looking at a map, the route was nowhere near where she lived and it wasn't as if the area was attractive. I was more than puzzled, I was intrigued.

The enquiry into the route of the new by-pass to the village was due to take place shortly, and I wanted to know what it was that **motivated** her. So it was that I found myself knocking on a cottage door, being received by Mary Smith and then being taken for a walk to the woods.

"I've always loved this place", she said, "it has a lot of memories for me, and for others. We all used it. They called it 'Lovers lane'. It's not much of a lane, and it doesn't go anywhere important, but that's why we all came here. To be away from people, to be by ourselves" she added.

It was indeed pleasant that day and the songs of many birds could be heard. Squirrels gazed from the branches, quite bold in their movements, **obviously** few people passed this way and they had nothing to fear. I could imagine the noise of vehicles passing through these peaceful woods when the by-pass was built, so I felt that she probably had something there but as I hold strong opinions about the needs of the community over-riding the opinions of private individuals, I said nothing. The village was quite a dangerous place because of the traffic especially for old people and children, their safety was more important to me than an old woman's whims.

"Take this tree", she said pausing after a short while. "To you it is just that, a tree. Not unlike many others here". She gently touched the bark. "Look here, under this branch, what can you see?"

"It looks as if someone has done a bit of carving with a knife" I said after a **cursory** inspection.

"Yes, that's what it is!" she said softly. "There are letters and a lover's heart".

I looked again, this time more carefully. The heart was still there and there was a suggestion of an arrow through it. The letters on one side were indistinct, but on the other an 'R' was clearly visible with what looked like an 'I' after it. "Some budding romance?" I asked, "did you know who they were?"

"Oh yes, I knew them", said Mary Smith, "it says RH loves MS".

I realized that I could be getting out of my depth, and longed to be in my office, away from here and this old lady, snug, and with a mug of tea in my hand.

She went on... "He had a penknife with a spike for getting stones from a horse's hoof, and I helped him to carve my **initials**. We were very much in love, but he was going away, and could not tell me what he was involved in the army. I had guessed of course. It was the last evening we ever spent together, because he went away the next day, back to his Unit."

Mary Smith was quiet for a while, then she sobbed. "His mother showed me the telegram. 'Sergeant R Holmes... Killed in action in the invasion of France'".

"'I had hoped that you and Robin would one day get married" she said, "He was my only child, and I would have loved to be a Granny, they would have been such lovely babies'—she was like that!"

"Two years later she too was dead. 'Pneumonia, following a chill on the chest' was what the doctor said, but I think it was an old fashioned broken heart. A child would have helped both of us."

There was a further pause. Mary Smith gently caressed the wounded tree, just as she would have caressed him. "And now they want to take our tree away from me." Another quiet sob, then she turned to me. "I was young and pretty then, I could have had anybody, I wasn't always the old woman you see here now. I had everything I wanted in life, a lovely man, health and a future to look forwards to".

She paused again and looked around. The breeze gently moved through the leaves with a sighing sound. "There were others, of course, but not a patch on my Robin!" she said strongly. "And now I have nothing—except the memories this tree holds. If only I could get my hands on that awful man who writes in the paper about the value of the road they are going to build where we are standing now, I would tell him, has he never loved, has he never lived, does he not know anything about memories? We were not the only ones, you know, I still meet some who came here as Robin and I did. Yes, I would tell him!"

I turned away, sick at heart.

赛斯汀

我实在不明白！为什么这个年老女士会对一片毫无用处的

老灌木林如此紧张呢？她给当地报纸写过信，甚至给全国性的报纸也写过信，对拟将在她们村子里修建道路的方案表示抗议。但从地图上看，这条拟建的小路离她家并不近，那一带的风景也不怎么优美。这不仅使我感到迷惑，还激起了我的好奇心。

很快就要进行对新道路的调查了，我想了解一下她反对的原因。于是我敲响了小屋的门，一位叫玛丽·史密斯的女士接待了我，然后她带我到了树林。

"我一直深爱着这个地方，"她说，"这里珍藏了我和其他许多人的回忆。我们都曾在这个地方呆过。人们称它为'情人路'。它其实并不能算是什么路，也不通往什么重要的地方，但这正是我们来这里的原因。远离他人，只有我们自己。"她补充说道。

那天林间实在迷人，小鸟唱着歌，松鼠在树枝间张望，自由自在，这里人迹罕至，它们一点都不害怕。我能想象得到，在道路修好后，汽车通过这片宁静的树林将会是怎样的喧闹，因此我猜这对她来说可能意味着些什么。但我坚持认为社区的需要重于个人的意见，所以我没说什么。村里目前的交通，特别是对于老人和小孩来说，尤其危险，所以对我来说他们的安全比这个老年女士的怪念头更为重要。

"拿这棵树来说吧，"她停了一会儿说，"对你来说它只是一棵普通的树，与这里其他的树没什么区别。"她轻轻地摸着树皮说："看这，在这个枝条下面，你看见了什么？"

"好像有人用小刀在这里刻过什么东西。"我看了一下说。

"是的，正是这样！"她轻轻地说，"是一些字母和一颗爱人的心。"

我又很仔细地看了看。刻的那颗心还在那，此外还依稀可以看见有支箭穿心而过。心一边的字母已无法辨认了，但在另一边，字母"R"清晰可见，后面还有个像是"I"的字母。"初恋罗曼史？"我问道，"你知道他们是谁吗？"

"唔，我知道。"玛丽·史密斯说，"写的是'RH 爱 MS'。"

我意识到我可能涉入太深了，真希望自己此刻身在办公室，远离这个地方和这个老年女士，手里还端着杯茶，舒舒服服地。

她继续讲着……"他拿着一把袖珍折刀，折刀上嵌有长钉，那种长钉可以用来挖出嵌在马蹄上的石块，我们一起刻了我名字的第一个字母。我们彼此相爱，但他却要离开了，而且也不知道他在军队里干什么。当然我也曾猜想过。那是我们在一起的最后一个夜晚，因为第二天他就回部队去了。"

玛丽·史密斯停了一会儿，接着抽泣了起来。"他母亲给我看了那封电报。'R·荷尔姆斯军士……在解放法国的战役中牺牲。'"

"我本来希望你和罗宾会结婚的。"她母亲说，"我只有他一个孩子，我本希望能做祖母，有非常可爱的小宝宝。"——她真是那么说的!

"两年后她也去世了。医生说是'肺炎，胸部着凉造成的'，但我认为这是典型的伤心过度。如果有个孩子，我们俩就都不会这样了。"

玛丽·史密斯又停了一会儿没说话。她轻柔地抚摸着那棵刻过的树，就像她曾经抚摸他那样。"现在他们想把我们的树夺走。"她又轻轻地抽噎了一下，然后她转过身对我说，"当时我年轻漂亮，我嫁给谁都可以，我当时可没有现在这么老。我拥有生命里所想要的一切，一个值得爱的男人、健康的身体和充满梦想的未来。"

她顿了顿，朝四周看了一眼。微风轻轻吹拂着树叶，发出叹息般的沙沙声。"当然，那时还有其他人，但他们连罗宾的一丝一毫都比不上!"她肯定地说。"现在我一无所有——只剩下残留在这棵树上的记忆。那个可恶的家伙竟建议把路修在我们所站的这个地方，我真想掐死他，我想问他：你从来没爱过吗，你活过吗，你不知道什么叫记忆吗？你知道吗，不仅仅是我们，现在我仍能看见些男男女女像当年的我和罗宾那样到这儿来。是的，我一定要对他说!"

我转过身去，心里觉得很难过。

Practising
& Exercise

核心单词

puzzled ['pʌzldəm] *adj.* 困惑的，茫然的

protest [prə'test] *v.* 抗议，反对

motivate ['məutiveit] *v.* 给……动机；刺激；激发

obviously ['ɔbvɪəslɪ] *adv.* 明显地；显然地

cursory [pɑː'teik] *adj.* 匆忙的；粗略的

initial [əi'niʃəl] *adj.* 开始的，最初的

实用句型

Why was this old woman making such a fuss about an old copse which was of no use to anybody?

为什么这个年老女士会对一片毫无用处的老灌木林如此紧张呢？

① which 在这里引导定语从句。

② make a fuss 大惊小怪，小题大作，另有 fuss over 过分关心等固定搭配。

翻译行不行

1. 你不如他仔细。(more than)

....

2. 由于健康问题，他不能参加会议。(due to)

....

3. 现在你看起来才像正常的你。(look like)

....

love Is More Thicker than Forget

爱情比忘却厚

· E.E.cummings ·

Love is more thicker than forget
More **thinner** than recall
More seldom than a wave is wet
More **frequent** than to fail

It is most mad and moonly
And less it shall unbe
Than all the sea which only
Is deeper than the sea

Love is less always than to win
Less never than **alive**
Less bigger than the least begin
Less littler than **forgive**

It is most **sane** and sunly
And more it cannot die
Than all the sky which only
Is higher than the sky

E·E·肯明斯

爱情比忘却厚
比回忆薄
比潮湿的波浪少
比失败多

它最痴癫最疯狂
但比起所有
比海洋更深的海洋
它更为长久

爱情总比胜利少见
却比活着多些
不大于无法开始
不小于谅解

它最明朗最清晰
而比起所有
比天空更高的天空
它更为不朽

Practising
& Exercise 实战
提升篇

核心单词

thinner ['θinə] *n.* 使变稀薄者；稀释剂

frequent ['fri:kwənt] *adj.* 频繁的；屡次的

alive [ə'laiv] *adj.* 有活力的，有生气的，活跃的

forgive [fə'giv] *v.* 原谅，宽恕

sane [sein] *adj.* 神志正常的，头脑清楚的；健全的

实用句型

Love is more thicker than forget. 爱情比忘却厚

①这是一个含有比较级的句子。

②thicker 更厚的,thick+er 构成了比较级形式,类似的词还有 tall ;short 等。

翻译行不行

1. 他对你的爱胜过一切。(deeper than)

....

2. 就仕途而言，他比你要走得远。(higher than)

....

3. 这个年轻人不到 20 岁。(less than)

....

Love Without Measure
爱无尺度

• Steve Goodier •

Freda Bright says: "Only in **opera** do people die for love." It's true. You really can't love somebody to death. I've known people to die from no love, but I've never known anyone to be loved to death. We just can't love one another enough.

A heart-warming story tells of a woman who finally decided to ask her boss for a raise in salary. All day she felt nervous and **apprehensive**. Late in the afternoon she summoned the courage to approach her employer. *To her delight, the boss agreed to a raise*.

The woman arrived home that evening to see a beautiful table set with their best dishes. Candles were softly glowing.

Her husband had come home early and prepared a festive meal. She wondered if someone from the office had tipped him off. Or... did he just somehow know that she would not get turned down?

She found him in the kitchen and told him the good news. They embraced and kissed, then sat down to the wonderful meal. Next to her plate the woman found a beautifully lettered note. It read: "Congratulations, darling! I knew you'd get the raise! These things will tell you how much I love you."

Following the supper, her husband went into the kitchen to clean up. She **noticed** that a second card had fallen from his pocket. Picking it up from the floor, she read: "Don't worry about not getting the raise! You deserve it anyway! These things will tell you how much I love you."

Someone has said that the measure of love is when you love without measure. What this man feels for his spouse is total acceptance and love, whether she succeeds or fails. His love **celebrates** her victories and soothes her wounds.

He stands with her, no matter what life throws in their direction. He may say that he loves her to death. But he doesn't. He loves her to LIFE. For his love nourishes her life like nothing else can.

Upon receiving the Nobel Peace Prize, Mother Teresa said: "What can you do to **promote** world peace? Go home and love your family." And love your friends. Love them without measure. Love them to LIFE.

斯蒂文·古蒂尔

弗里达·布莱特说过："只有在戏剧中，人们才会为爱而死。"确实，你真的不可能爱一个人到死。我知道人们会因为得不到爱去死，但我没听说过有谁会被爱死。我们只是觉得无论如何相爱都还不够。

有一个温馨的故事，讲一个女人终于决定向老板提出加薪的请求。一整天，她都忧心忡忡的，直到晚上快下班时，她终于鼓足勇气去跟老板说，令她高兴的是，老板同意给她加薪。

那天晚上，当女人回到家时，她看到漂亮的餐桌上烛光闪烁，摆满了佳肴。

她的丈夫提前回到家准备了庆祝晚宴。她纳闷是不是办公室里有人给他透漏了消息。或者……他怎么知道她不会被拒绝？

她到厨房找到他并且告诉他这个好消息。他们相拥并亲吻，然后坐下来享受美味的晚餐。女人在她盘子旁边发现了一张字迹优美的小纸条，写着：祝贺你，亲爱的！我知道你会加薪的！这些都将告诉你我有多爱你。

晚饭后，丈夫去厨房收拾，女人注意到从他口袋里掉出了一张小卡片。她从地板上捡了起来，卡片上写着：别去为没加薪而烦恼！你完全有资格加薪。这些都将告诉你我有多爱你。

有人说，爱的尺度就是无尺度地去爱。这个男人给予妻子的是完全的包容和爱，不管妻子是成功还是失败。他的爱可以为她庆祝胜利，也可以为她抚平创伤。

无论他们的生活怎样，他们始终同舟共济。他也许会说他爱她爱到死，其实他不是，他是爱她到"生"，因为没有什么能像他的爱这样去丰富她的生命。

特蕾莎修女在接受诺贝尔和平奖时说道："你怎样能促进世界和平呢？回家爱你的家人吧。"此外，还要爱你的朋友，无尺度地去爱他们吧。爱他们到"生"。

核心单词

opera ['ɔpərə] *n.* 歌剧；歌剧艺术

apprehensive [ˌæpri'hensiv] *adj.* 忧虑的，恐惧的

notice ['nəutis] *n.* 公告，通知，贴示

celebrate ['selibreit] *v.* 庆祝；颂扬，赞美

promote [prə'məut] *v.* 晋升；促进；发扬

实用句型

To her delight，the boss agreed to a raise.

令她高兴的是，老板同意给她加薪。

① to 引导的短语，表"为了……"。

② agree to 同意，类似的表达还有 agree upon 对……取得一致意见；agree with 和……意见一致等固定搭配。

翻译行不行

1. 有人泄密给罪犯，他就逃走了。(tip off)

....

2. 我会调查这事的。(go into)

....

3. 我们应该清理逾期票据。(clean up)

....

Late at Night, Do You Turn off Your Cell Phone?
深夜，你关机了吗？

· Anonymous ·

The girl would turn her cell phone off and put it by her photo on the desk every night before going to bed. This habit has been with her ever since she bought the phone.

The girl had a very close boyfriend. When they couldn't meet, they would either call or send messages to each other. They both liked this type of **communication**.

One night, the boy really missed the girl. When he called her, however, the girl's cell phone was off because she was already asleep. The next day, the boy asked the girl to leave her cell phone on at night because when he needed to find her and could not, he would be worried.

From that day forth, the girl began a new habit. Her cell phone never shuts down at night. Because she was afraid that she might not be able to hear the phone ring in her sleep, she tried to stay very **alert**. As days passed, she became thinner and thinner. Slowly, a gap began to form between them.

The girl wanted to revive their relationship. On one night, she called the boy. However, what she got was a sweet **female** voice: "Sorry, the subscriber you dailed is power off."

The girl knew that her love has just been turned off.

After a long time, the girl has a new love. *No matter how well they got along, the girl however refused to get married.* In the girl's heart, she always remembered that boy's words and the night when that phone was power off.

The girl still keeps the habit of leaving her cell phone on all throughout the night, but not expecting that it'll ring.

One night, the girl caught ill. In moment of **fluster**, instead of calling her parents, she dialed the new boy's cell phone. The boy was already asleep but his cell phone was still on.

Later, the girl asked the boy: "Why don't you turn your cell phone off at night?"

The boy answered: "I'm afraid that if you need anything at night and aren't able to find me, you'll worry."

The girl **finally** married the boy.

佚　名

女孩每晚在睡觉前都会先关掉手机，然后把它放在写字台上自己的相架前，这个习惯从买了手机开始就这样保持着。

女孩有个很亲密的男朋友，在两个人无法见面的时候，就打电话或发短信，他们都喜欢这样的联络方式。

有一天夜里，男孩很想念女孩，打了电话过去却发现已经关机，因为女孩已经睡了。第二天，男孩对女孩说："以后晚上不要关机，好吗？我想你的时候却找不到你，我的心会不安。"

从那以后，女孩养成了一个新习惯——整夜都不关机。因为害怕男孩打电话来自己睡得太熟而听不到，女孩夜夜都很警醒，长此以往，人也日渐消瘦。然而，慢慢地，两个人之间还是有了裂痕。

女孩很想挽回这段感情，便在一个深夜里给男孩打电话，她听到的却是一个甜美的女声："对不起，你所拨打的电话已关机。"

于是女孩知道，她的爱情已经关机了。

很久以后，女孩有了另一场爱情。虽然两个人在一起的感觉也很好，但女孩怎么也不肯嫁给他。因为女孩经常会想起那个男孩的话和那个关机的夜。

女孩还是保持着整夜不关机的习惯，只是不再期待它会响起。

一天夜里，女孩身染急症，慌乱之中把本想拨给父母的电话拨到了新男友那里。男孩早已睡下，但手机还开着。

后来女孩问这个男孩："为什么深夜还不关机？"

男孩说："我怕你夜里有事找不到我，会心慌。"

女孩最终嫁给了这个男孩。

Practising
& Exercise

核心单词

communication [kə,mju:ni'keiʃn] *n.* 传达；交流；通信
alert [ə'lə:t] *adj.* 警觉的；警惕的；留神的
female ['fi:meil] *adj.* 女（性）的；雌的
fluster ['flʌstə] *n.* 慌乱；激动 *v.* 使激动
finally ['fainəli] *adv.* 最后，终于

实用句型

No matter how well they got along，the girl however refused to get married.

虽然两个人在一起的感觉也很好，但女孩怎么也不肯嫁给他。

①这是由 no matter 引导的条件状语从句。

② get along 和睦相处，类似的表达还有 get over 克服；get out 泄漏；get off 动身等固定搭配。

翻译行不行

1. 离开前请把灯关掉。（turn off）

....

2. 我将代你去。（instead of）

....

3. 你很快就会知道真相了。（be able to）

....

Say "I Love You"
大声说出你的爱

• Matthew •

There was once a guy who suffered from cancer, a cancer that can't be **cured**. He was 18 years old and he could die anytime. All his life, he was stuck in his house being taken care of by his mother. He never went outside but he was sick of staying home and wanted to go out for once. So he asked his mother and she gave him **permission**.

He walked down his block and found a lot of stores. He passed a CD store and looked through the front door for a second as he walked. He stopped and went back to look into the store. He saw a beautiful girl about his age and he knew it was love at first sight. He opened the door and walked in, not looking at anything else but her. He walked closer and closer until he was finally at the front desk where she sat.

She looked up and asked, "Can I help you?"

She smiled and he thought it was the most beautiful smile he has ever seen before and wanted to kiss her right there.

He said, "Uh... Yeah... Umm... I would like to buy a CD."

He picked one out and gave her money for it.

"Would you like me to **wrap** it for you?" she asked, smiling her cute smile again.

He nodded and she went to the back. She came back with the wrapped CD and gave it to him. He took it and walked out of the store.

He went home and from then on, he went to that store every day and bought a CD, and she wrapped it for him. He took the CD home and put it in his closet. He was still too shy to ask her out and he really wanted to but he couldn't. His mother found out about this and told him to just ask her. So the next day, he took all his courage and went to the store as usual. He bought a CD like he did every day and once again she went to the back of the store and came back with it wrapped. He took it and when she wasn't looking, he left his phone number on the desk and ran out...

RRRRRING!!!

One day the phone rang, and the mother picked it up and said, "Hello?" It was the girl!!! The mother started to cry and said, "You don't know? He passed away yesterday..."

The line was quiet except for the cries of the boy's mother. Later in the day, the mother went into the boy's room because she wanted to remember him. She thought she would start by looking at his clothes. So she opened the **closet**.

She was face to face with piles and piles and piles of unopened CDs. She was surprised to find all these CDs and she picked one up and sat down on the bed and she started to open one. Inside, there was a CD and as she took it out of the wrapper, out fell a piece of paper. The mother picked it up and

我希望有人在什么地方等我

started to read it. It said: Hi... I think U R **really** cute. Do u wanna go out with me? Love, Jocelyn.

The mother was deeply moved and opened another CD...Again there was a piece of paper. It said: Hi... I think U R really cute. Do u wanna go out with me? Love, Jocelyn.

Love is... when you've had a huge **fight** but then decide to put aside your **egos**, hold hands and say, "I Love You."

马 修

从前，有一个少年患了根本无法治愈的癌症。18 岁的他随时都面临着死亡的威胁。他每天都待在家里，由母亲照料着，从未出过家门，在家实在待烦了，便征得母亲的同意出去走走。

走在大街上，他看到很多商店。当路过 家音像店时，他情不自禁地透过橱窗向里望了望，他停下脚步，又转身折回店门，向里望去。一个与他年龄相仿的，漂亮可爱的女孩子引起了他的注意；并对她一见钟情。他打开门，走了进去，他的眼里始终只有那女孩一个人。他不由自主地走到了柜台前，走到那个女孩坐着的地方。

女孩抬头问道："请问，您需要什么？"

她微笑着，他觉得这是他一生中所见到的最迷人的笑容，其实此时他最想做的就是亲吻她。

他说："是的，嗯，那个……我想买一张 CD。"

他随便拿了张 CD，连同钱一起递给了她。

"我给你包起来吧？"女孩问，又冲他露出了迷人的微笑。

他点了点头。她又回到柜台后面。出来时，把包装好的CD交给了他。他接过来，走出了商店。

他回家了。自那以后，他每天都要去那家音像店买一张CD。女孩每次都会给他包好，而他每次把CD拿回家，都放到壁橱里。他很害羞，没有勇气约她出去，他真的很想那么做，但却做不到。母亲知道后，不断地鼓励他。第二天，他终于鼓起了勇气，像往常一样走进了那家音像店，买了一张CD，她也像往常一样，到柜台后把CD包了起来。他接过CD，趁她不注意时他将自己的电话号码放在柜台上，然后跑了出去……

叮铃铃铃!!!

一天，电话铃响了起来，母亲接起电话说："喂，您好！"是那个女孩打来的!!! 母亲伤心地哭了，她说："你知道吗？他昨天"走"了……"

电话那端沉默了片刻，只能听到母亲的啜泣声。后来，母亲到儿子的房间去，她只是想念儿子了，想看看他的衣服，于是打开了壁橱。

一大堆包好的CD映入了母亲的眼帘，这些CD都没有拆开过。母亲感到很吃惊，她好奇地打开一个包装，从中取出CD，一张小纸条从里面掉了出来，她捡了起来，看到上面这样写着：嗨,你好吗？我觉得你真的好可爱,愿意和我一起出去吗？爱你的乔斯林。

母亲被深深地感动了，她打开了另一个CD盒……也有一张小纸条，上面写着同样的话：嗨,你好吗？我觉得你真的好可爱，愿意和我一起出去吗？爱你的乔斯林。

爱就是在你做了巨大的思想斗争之后，最终决定舍弃自我，面对爱人，攥紧手，说出"我爱你"。

核心单词

cure [kjuə] v. 治愈

permission [pə(:)'miʃən] n. 允许，许可，同意

wrap [ræp] v. 包，裹；缠绕

closet ['klɔzit] n. 壁橱；碗橱；衣橱

really ['riəli] adv. 真地，确实，实际上

fight [fait] v. 打仗；打架；奋斗

ego ['i:gəu] n. 自我；自我意识

实用句型

There was once a guy who suffered from cancer, a cancer that can't be cured. 从前，有一个少年患了癌症，根本无法治愈。

①这里是由 who 引导的定语从句。

②suffer from 因（疾病）而痛或不舒服，类似的表达还有 suffer for 遭受痛苦，受损失等。

翻译行不行

1. 她常常头痛。（suffer from）

......

2. 从那时起，王子与公主就幸福地生活在一起了。（from then on）.

......

3. 他把工作暂时搁下以便有更多时间陪儿子。（put aside）

......

Love Is Just A Thread
爱如丝线

• Wesley •

Sometimes I really doubt whether there is love between my parents. Every day they are very busy trying to earn money in order to pay the high tuition for my brother and me. They don't act in the romantic ways that I read in books or I see on TV. In their opinion, "I love you" is too luxurious for them to say. Sending flowers to each other on Valentine's Day is even more out of the question. Finally my father has a bad temper. When he's very tired from the hard work, it is easy for him to lose his temper.

One day, my mother was sewing a **quilt**. I silently sat down beside her and looked at her.

"Mom, I have a question to ask you," I said after a while.

"What?" she replied, still doing her work.

"Is there love between you and Dad?" I asked her in a very low voice.

My mother stopped her work and raised her head with **surprise** in her eyes. She didn't answer immediately. Then she bowed her head and continued to sew the quilt.

I was very worried because I thought I had hurt her. I was in great **embarrassment** and I didn't know what I should do. But at last I heard my mother say the following words:

"Susan," she said thoughtfully, "look at this thread. *Sometimes it appears, but most of it disappears in the quilt.* The **thread** really makes the quilt strong and **durable**. If life is a quilt, then love should be a thread. It can hardly be seen anywhere or anytime, but it's really there. Love is inside."

I listened carefully but I couldn't understand her until the next spring. At that time, my father suddenly got sick **seriously**. My mother had to stay with him in the hospital for a month. When they returned from the hospital, they both looked very pale. It seemed both of them had had a serious illness.

After they were back, every day in the morning and dusk, my mother helped my father walk slowly on the country road. My father had never been so gentle. It seemed they were the most harmonious couple. Along the country road, there were many beautiful flowers, green grass and trees. The sun gently glistened through the leaves. All of these made up the most beautiful picture in the world.

The doctor had said my father would **recover** in two months. But after two months he still couldn't walk by himself. All of us were worried about him.

"Dad, how are you feeling now?" I asked him one day.

"Susan, don't worry about me." he said gently. "To tell you the truth, I just like walking with your mom. I like this kind of life." Reading his eyes, I know he loves my mother deeply.

Once I thought love meant flowers, gifts and sweet kisses.

But from this experience, I understand that love is just a thread in the quilt of our life. Love is **inside**, making life strong and warm.

卫斯理

　　有时我怀疑，父母之间是否存在着真爱。他们每天都疲于奔命，为我和弟弟赚学费。我从没见他们像我在书中或电视中看到的那样浪漫。在他们看来，将"我爱你"这句话说出口都太奢侈，更别说在情人节互赠鲜花了。父亲脾气很暴，特别是在下班回家后，他很容易发脾气。

　　有一天，妈妈正在缝被子，我安静地坐在旁边看着她。

　　"妈妈，我有个问题想问你。"过了一会儿我说。

　　"什么问题啊？"她答道，而手里的活儿却没停下。

　　"你和爸爸之间有爱情吗？"我压低声音问道。

　　母亲停下了手里的活儿，抬起头诧异地看着我，她并未马上回答，然后又低下头，继续缝被子。

　　我担心这个问题伤她的心了。我很尴尬，不知所措。但接下来却听见母亲这样说：

　　"苏珊，"她若有所思地说，"你看这线。有时我们看得见它，但更多时候它却藏在被子中，我们看不见。但这些线却使被子结实耐用。如果将生活比做被子，那么爱就是丝线。你不可能时刻都看得到它，但是它却真实地存在着。爱是内在的东西。"

　　我仔细听着，但是直到第二年春天才真正明白她所说的话。

当时，父亲突然病重，母亲在医院里照顾他，当父亲在一个月后出院回到家时，他们两个人的脸色都很苍白，就像得过同样的重病似的。

他们回家后，每到黎明和黄昏，母亲总会搀扶着父亲在乡间小路上散步。父亲从没有那样温和过。他们看起来是那样和谐。路旁有许多漂亮的鲜花、绿草和树木，阳光透过叶子的缝隙温柔地照射在上面，所有这一切勾勒出了世间最美的画面。

医生说，两个月后父亲就能病愈。可两个月后他还是不能独立行走，我们都很担心。

"你感觉如何，爸爸？"有一天我问他。

"苏珊，不要担心我。"父亲慢慢地说，"不瞒你说，我就是喜欢和你妈妈一起散步的感觉。我喜欢这样的生活。"从他的眼神中，我读出了他对母亲那深深的爱恋。

曾经以为爱情是与鲜花、礼物和香甜的热吻这些美好的事物分不开的。但经历了这些后，我明白了：爱情就如同我们生活中被子里的丝线一样，是内在的、坚固和温暖生活的东西。

Practising & Exercise 实战 提升篇

核心单词

quilt [kwilt] *n.* 被（子）；被褥

surprise [sə'praiz] *n.* 惊奇，诧异

embarrassment [im'bærəsmənt] *n.* 窘；难堪

thread [θred] *n.* 线；线状物

durable ['djuərəbl] *adj.* 经久的，耐用的

seriously ['siəriəsli] *adv.* 严肃地；认真地；当真地

recover [ri'kʌvə] *v.* 重新获得；重新找到；恢复

inside ['in'said] *n.* 内部，里面

实用句型

Sometimes it appears，but most of it disappears in the quilt.

有时我们看得见它，但更多时候它却藏在被子中，我们看不见。

①在这句中用了 appears–disappears 这对反义词，以表强调。

②disappear 消失，不见，类似的词还有 disable 使丧失能力；disabled 残疾的等。

翻译行不行

1. 他们终于到达了上海。(at last)

2. 我岳母这星期同我们住在一起。(stay with)

3. 这个故事完全是虚构出来的。(make up)

True Love Always Prevails over All
真爱超越一切

• Benjamin Reinemund •

True love is we stick together in "thick and thin", especially when it's thin, when it's troublesome. Then we should really **bridge** over the "troubled water". That's what they say in English. But most of us fail the test, to ourselves, not to our partners. He might leave you ; he might stay with you, because you're nice or not nice. But you fail yourself. You leave yourself. You leave the noblest being that you really are. So we should check up on this to our family members or whomever that is beloved and dear to us. Most of the time in **critical** situations, we just turn our backs and that is not good.

Of course we have our anger, our frustrations, because our partners are not as loving as usual, or whomever that is ; but he or she is in a different situation. At that time, she or he is in mental suffering. *It's just as bad or even worse than physical suffering*. For physical suffering you can take a pill or you can have an **injection** and it stops or at least temporarily stops, and you feel the effect right away ; or at least if people are in physical suffering, everyone sympathizes with them.

But when they are in mental **anguish**, and we pound them more on that, and we turn our backs and become cold and indifferent, that is even crueler, even worse. That person will be swimming alone in suffering. And especially they trust us as the next of kin, the next person, the one that they think they can rely on in times of need ; and then at that time, we just turn around and are **snobbish**, because they didn't treat us nice so we just want to revenge. That's not the time. You can **revenge** later, when he's in better shape. Just slap him.

Actually, at that time, the person is not his usual self anymore. He was probably under very great pressure that he lost his own control. It's not really that lost his own control, but for example, when you are in a hurry, your talk is different, Right? "Hand me that coat ! Quick ! Quick! Quick!" Things like that. But **normally,** you would say "Honey, please, can you give me that coat." Is that not so? Or when you're in pain—for example stomach pain, heartache or whatever—you scream loudly ; and anyone who comes to talk to you, you don't talk in the usual way anymore, because you're in pain.

Similarly, when you are in a mental or psychological pain, you talk also in a very grouchy way, very cross. But that is understandable. So if we—any so-called loving partner or family member—do not understand even this very least, very basic **concept**, then we're finished. Then we are really in a bad situation. It's not that the partner will do anything to us. Whether he does anything to us later or not, that is no problem. The problem is us. The problem is we degrade ourselves, that we make less of a being of ourselves than we should be, than we are supposed to be, or that we really are. So do not make less of a being of yourselves.

本杰明·雷蒙德

真爱是不管处境好与不好都应该在一起的，特别是当处境不好、有麻烦时，更应该"同甘共苦"，但对于我们自己来讲，大部分人都无法做到这一点，而不是我们的同伴做不到。由于你的热情，他会与你同甘共苦，或由于你的冷漠，他会离你而去。是你背弃了自己，背弃了本应高尚的自我。所以我们应该反省自己对家人或任何我们所钟爱的人的关系，通常是在关键的时刻我们背弃了他们，这样很不好。

当然我们也会生气、失望，因为我们的伴侣不再像以前一样可爱，不过这是因为他（她）正处在不同的时期，也许精神正饱受煎熬。精神上的痛苦和肉体上的折磨，有时是一样的，有时则更甚。肉体的痛苦可以藉吃药或打针来制止，至少可以暂时止痛，可以马上见效。因为在经历病痛时，大家都会表示同情。

可是当有人心理极度痛苦时，我们却落井下石，背弃他，或变得冷漠不关心，这更残忍、更糟糕。那个人就只能孤孤单单地在痛苦中挣扎。尤其是当他们把我们当作是最亲密的人，认为在需要时可以依靠，可是就在那时，我们却因为他们对我们的不友好或是想报复她而势利地转身而去。这可真不是时候！

你可以等一下再报复，等他好一点时，再打他一巴掌。

事实上，那时候那个人已经不再是平常的他，对我们的不友好可能是因压力极大而失去自控造成的，也可能并非是完全失去了控制。就像你在匆忙时，说话的语气就会不同与往常，你会说："把外衣给我，快快快！"而你平常都会说："亲爱的，能不能把那件外衣给我？"是不是这样？或当你在痛苦时，比如在你的胃或头疼痛难忍时，你跟来人也无法像平常那样谈话，因为你正痛得不得了。

同理，当你精神低迷或心情郁闷时，你的谈话自然会显得粗暴，但这是可以理解的。如果我们这些所谓的亲爱的伴侣或家人不知道这是最起码、最基本的观念，我们的处境会很尴尬。并非另一半会对我们怎样，无论对方以后有没有对我们怎样，那都不是问题，问题在于我们自己——是我们自己低估了自己，而非真正有的自我，所以千万不要小看自己。

核心单词

bridge [bridʒ] *n.* 桥，桥梁

critical ['krɪtɪkəl] *adj.* 紧要的，关键性的，危急的

injection [in'dʒekʃən] *n.* 注射；注射剂

anguish ['æŋgwiʃ] *n.* 极度的痛苦；苦恼

snobbish ['snɔbiʃ] *adj.* 势利眼的

revenge [ri'vendʒ] *v.* 替……报仇；报复，洗雪

normally ['nɔ:məli] *adv.* 正常地；通常，按惯例

concept ['kɔnsept] *n.* 概念，观念，思想

实用句型

It's just as bad or even worse than physical suffering.

精神上的痛苦和肉体上的折磨，有时是一样的，有时则更甚。

①这是一个比较句，as 连接同级比较，than 差级比较。

②as...as 和……一样，类似的表达还有 so...as。

翻译行不行

1. 请核对一下这些数据。(check up)

......

2. 她早餐照样吃面包和鸡蛋。(as usual)

......

3. 她男朋友离她而去，使她痛苦万分。(in pain)

......

The Best Kind of Love
天底下最真挚的爱情

· Phoebe ·

I have a friend who is falling in love. She **honestly** claims the
sky is bluer. Mozart moves her to tears. She has lost 15 pounds
and looks like a cover girl.

"I'm young again!" she shouts **exuberantly**.

As my friend raves on about her new love, I've taken
a good look at my old one. My husband of almost 20 years,
Scott, has gained 15 pounds. Once a marathon runner, he
now runs only down hospital halls. His hairline is receding
and his body shows the signs of long working hours and too
many candy bars. Yet he can still give me a certain look across a
restaurant table and I want to ask for the **check** and head home.

When my friend asked me "What will make this love
last?" I ran through all the obvious reasons: commitment,
shared interests, unselfishness, physical attraction,
communication. Yet there's more. We still have fun.
Spontaneous good times. Yesterday, after slipping the rubber
band off the rolled up newspaper, Scott flipped it playfully at
me: this led to an all-out war. Last Saturday at the **grocery**,
we split the list and raced each other to see who could make it

to the checkout first. Even washing dishes can be a blast. We enjoy simply being together.

And there are surprises. One time I came home to find a note on the front door that led me to another note, then another, until I reached the walk-in closet. I opened the door to find Scott holding a "pot of gold" (my cooking kettle) and the "treasure" of a gift **package**. Sometimes I leave him notes on the mirror and little presents under his pillow.

There is understanding. I understand why he must play basketball with the guys. And he understands why, once a year, I must get away from the house, the kids—and even him—to meet my sisters for a few days of nonstop talking and laughing.

There is sharing. *Not only do we share household worries and parental burdens—we also share ideas.* Scott came home from a convention last month and presented me with a thick historical novel. Though he prefers thrillers and science fiction, he had read the novel on the plane. He touched my heart when he explained it was because he wanted to be able to exchange ideas about the book after I'd read it.

There is forgiveness. When I'm embarrassingly loud and crazy at parties, Scott forgives me. When he **confessed** losing some of our savings in the stock market, I gave him a hug and said, "It's okay. It's only money."

There is sensitivity. Last week he walked through the door with that look that tells me it's been a tough day. After he spent some time with the kids, I asked him what happened. He told me about a 60-year-old woman who'd had a stroke. He wept as he recalled the woman's husband standing beside her bed, caressing her hand. How was he going to tell this husband of 40 years that his wife would probably never recover? I shed a few tears myself. Because of the medical crisis. Because there were still people who have been married 40 years. Because my husband is still moved and **concerned** after years of hospital rooms and dying patients.

There is faith. Last Tuesday a friend came over and confessed her fear that her husband is losing his courageous battle with cancer. On Wednesday I went to lunch with a friend who is struggling to reshape her life after divorce. On Thursday a neighbor called to talk about the frightening effects of Alzheimer's disease on her father-in-law's personality. On Friday a child-hood friend called long-distance to tell me her father had died. I hung up the phone and thought ; this is too much heartache for one week. Through my tears, as I went out to run some errands, I noticed the **boisterous** orange blossoms of the gladiolus outside my window. I heard the delighted laughter of my son and his friend as they played. I caught sight of a wedding party emerging from a neighbor's house. The bride, dressed in satin and lace, tossed her bouquet to her cheering friends. That night, I told my husband about these events. We helped each other acknowledge the cycles of life and that the joys counter the sorrows. It was enough to keep us going.

Finally, there is knowing. I know Scott will throw his laundry just shy of the hamper every night ; he'll be late to most appointments and eat the last chocolate in the box. He knows that I sleep with a pillow over my head ; I'll lock us out of the house at a regular basis, and I will also eat the last chocolate.

I guess our love lasts because it is comfortable. No, the sky is not bluer: it's just a familiar hue. We don't feel particularly young: we've experienced too much that has contributed to our growth and wisdom, taking its toll on our bodies, and created our memories.

I hope we've got what it takes to make our love last. As a bride, I had Scott's wedding band **engraved** with Robert Browning's line "Grow old along with me!" We're following those instructions.

菲　比

　　我一个朋友正处于热恋中，她幸福地坦言，恋爱时，天空似乎更蓝了。莫扎特的音乐让她感动得落泪。恋爱使她的体重减轻了15磅，她看起来像个封面女郎。

　　"我又年轻了！"她兴奋地喊道。

　　在朋友对她的新欢赞不绝口时，我又重新审视我的旧爱。丈夫斯科特和我结婚快20年了，他的体重增加了15磅，曾是马拉松选手的他，如今却只能从楼上跑到楼下的医院大厅。他的发际线不断后移。从体形可以看出，他经常超负荷地工作，并且甜食吃得太多。但约会时，餐桌对面的他仍会向我使某种眼神，我便心领神会，结账回家。

　　当朋友问我"是什么使你们的爱持续至今"时，我毫不犹豫地列举了一些显性因素：责任感、共同的兴趣爱好、无私、身体吸引力，再有就是沟通。当然，还有其他诸多因素：我们会时常寻找乐趣，共度欢乐时光。昨天，斯科特把捆报纸的橡皮筋拉下来，然后调皮地弹向我，"战争"由此一发不可收拾；上周六在杂货店，我们把购物单一分为二，比赛看谁先抢购完到达收银台，谁就是胜利者；即便是一起洗碗，我们也要打斗一番。只要在一起，我们就开心。

我们常会给对方带来惊喜。一次，我回到家，发现门上贴着一张小纸条，它指引我找到了另一张纸条，接着又一张，最后指引我走到小储藏室。我打开门，发现斯科特手里捧着"金罐子"（我的蒸煮锅），还拿着一个装着"财富"的大礼包。有时我也会把给他的纸条贴在镜子上，偷偷地在他的枕头下藏一个小礼物。

我们都理解对方。我理解他为什么一定要和老朋友出去打篮球，而他也理解我为什么每年都要离开他和孩子，去与姐妹们聚会，连续几天，无休止地说说笑笑。

我们同甘共苦。不仅分担家事的忧愁和身为父母的责任，也分享各自的见解。上个月，斯科特参加了一个会议，给我带回一本很厚的历史小说。虽然他比较喜欢惊悚和科幻小说，但他还是在飞机上把它读完了。他说是为了在我读完后，能和我交流见解。听了这番话，我感动不已。

我们彼此宽容。当我在派对上不顾一切，疯狂地喧闹时，斯科特原谅了我。而当他用我们的一点积蓄炒股赔了钱，并向我坦白时，我抱紧他，安慰道："没关系，钱乃身外之物。"

我们心有灵犀。上周，他回家，一进门我便从他的神情看出，他今天过得很不开心。他逗孩子们玩了一会儿后，我问他怎么了。他告诉我，一个60岁的老太太中风了。想到病人的丈夫站在床边爱抚她的手时，他哭了。他实在不忍心告诉病人的丈夫，与他共度了40年的妻子可能永远不能康复！我的眼泪也流了下来，为那可恶的病魔，为这世间还有维系40年的婚姻，也为丈夫这么多年来在医院目睹了无数垂死的病人后还能有如此的感动和怜悯!

我们都有坚定的信念。上周二,一个朋友到我家来,向我诉说了她的忧虑,她担心丈夫逐渐丧失与癌症抗争的勇气和信心。周三,我和一个朋友吃午饭,她正努力使离婚后的生活步入正轨。周四,一个邻居打电话告诉我,可怕的老年痴呆症困扰着她公公。周五,小时候和我一起玩的一个伙伴打来长途电话来通告他父亲去世的噩耗。我放下电话,心想,一周内竟连续发生这么多令人揪心的悲剧。泪水模糊了我的双眼。我走出家门,想做点什么,却发现窗外橙色的剑兰花竟开了,儿子和伙伴们玩耍的欢声笑语传到耳边,邻居正在举办婚宴,新娘子穿着缎面有花边修饰的婚纱,把花束抛向欢呼雀跃的朋友。那一夜,我把这一切都讲给丈夫听,我们相互慰藉。人生轮回、悲欢离合总会伴随我们,我们将这样相濡以沫地生活下去。

最后一个原因,我们互相了解。我知道斯科特每晚都会把换洗的衣服扔向洗衣篓,却总也扔不进去;我知道多数约会他都会迟到,因而会被罚吃剩下的最后一块巧克力。他知道我睡觉时喜欢用枕头把头蒙起来,我时常忘带钥匙,进不了家门,因此我也会自觉地吃掉最后一块巧克力。

我猜想,或许是舒适的感觉让我们的爱延续至今。天空和昨天一样。并没有变得更蓝,它仍是我们熟悉的颜色;我们也不再有年轻的感觉:我们经历的太多了,而正是这些经历使我们成长,让我们更理性,使我们不断增值,构成了我们的回忆。

我希望我们已经得到了使爱情延续的秘诀。结婚时,斯科特在我的戒指上刻上了罗伯特·布朗宁的诗词:"陪我到老吧!"我们始终恪守着这一誓言。

核心单词

honestly [ˈɔnistli] *adv.* 诚实地，如实地；公正地

exuberantly [igˈzju:bəreit] *adv.* 丰富地；繁茂地

check [tʃek] *n.* 检查，检验，核对

grocery [ˈɡrəusəri] *n.* 食品杂货店

package [ˈpækidʒ] *n.* 包裹；包；包装箱

confess [kənˈfes] *v.* 坦白，供认，承认

concerned [kənˈsə:nd] *adj.* 挂虑的，担心的，不安的

boisterous [ˈbɔistərəs] *adj.* 喧闹的；爱闹的；狂欢的

engraved [inˈɡreivd] *adj.* 被深深印入的；被牢记的

实用句型

Not only do we share household worries and parental burdens—we also share ideas.

不仅分担家事的忧愁和身为父母的责任，也分享各自的见解。

① Not only 放在句首时，后面的句子要用部分倒装。

② not only...but also 在使用中经常用它的省略形式 not only...but。

翻译行不行

1. 我已经要求增援了。(ask for)

....

2. 我要把这份报表很快看一遍。(run through)

....

3. 我看见她匆忙走开，但我并没有跟她讲话。(catch sight of)

....

A Good Heart to Lean on
善心可依

· Anonymous ·

When I was growing up, I was **embarrassed** to be seen with my father. He was severely crippled and very short, and when we would walk together, his hand on my arm for balance, people would stare. I would inwardly squirm at the unwanted attention. If he ever noticed or was bothered, he never let on.

It was difficult to coordinate our steps—his **halting**, mine impatient — and because of that, we didn't say much as we went along. But as we started out, he always said, "You set the pace. I will try to adjust to you."

Our usual walk was to or from the subway, which was how he got to work. He went to work sick, and despite nasty weather. He almost never missed a day, and would make it to the office even if others could not. A matter of pride.

When snow or ice was on the ground, it was impossible for him to walk, even with help. At such times my sisters or I would pull him through the streets of Brooklyn, NY, on a child's **sleigh** to the subway entrance. Once there, he would cling to the handrail until he reached the lower steps that the warmer tunnel air kept ice-free. In Manhattan the subway station was the basement of his office building, and he would not have to go outside again until we met him in Brooklyn'on his way home.

When I think of it now, I marvel at how much courage it must have taken for a grown man to subject himself to such **indignity** and stress. And at how he did it—without bitterness or complaint .

He never talked about himself as an object of pity, nor did he show any envy of the more fortunate or able. What he looked for in others was a "good heart", and if he found one, the owner was good enough for him.

Now that I am older, I believe that is a proper standard by which to judge people, even though I still don't know **precisely** what a "good heart" is. But I know the times I don't have one myself.

Unable to engage in many activities, my father still tried to participate in some way. When a local sandlot baseball team found itself without a manager, he kept it going. He was a knowledgeable baseball fan and often took me to Ebbets Field to see the Brooklyn Dodgers play. He liked to go to dances and parties, where he could have a good time just sitting and watching.

On one memorable occasion a fight broke out at a beach party, with everyone punching and shoving. He wasn't content to sit and watch, but he couldn't stand unaided on the soft sand. In **frustration** he began to shout, "I'll fight anyone who will sit down with me!" Nobody did. But the next day people kidded him by saying it was the first time any fighter was urged to take a dive even before the bout began.

I now know he participated in some things vicariously through me，his only son. When I played ball (poorly)，he "played" too. When I joined the Navy he "joined" too. And when I came home on leave, he saw to it that I visited his office. Introducing me, he was really saying, "This is my son, but it is also me, and I could have done this, too, if things had been different." Those words were never said **aloud**.

He has been gone many years now, but I think of him often. I wonder if he sensed my reluctance to be seen with him during our walks. If he did, I am sorry I never told him how sorry I was, how unworthy I was, how I regretted it. I think of him when I complain about **trifles**, when I am envious of another's good fortune, when I don't have a "good heart".

佚　名

　　在我成长的过程中，我一直羞于让别人看见我和父亲在一起。我的父亲身材矮小，腿上有严重的残疾。当我们一起走路时，他总是挽着我以保持身体平衡，这时总招来一些异样的目光，令我无地自容。可是如果他注意到了这些，不管他内心多么痛苦，也从不表现出来。

走路时，我们很难相互协调起来——他的步子慢慢腾腾，我的步子焦躁不安。所以一路上我们交谈得很少。但是每次出行前，他总是说，"你走你的，我尽量跟上你。"

我们常常往返于从家到他上班乘坐的地铁站的那段路上。他有病也要上班，不管天气多么恶劣。他几乎从没误过一天工，就是在别人不能去的情况下，他也要设法去上班。实在值得骄傲！

每当冰封大地，雪花飘飘的时候，若是没有帮助，他简直举步维艰。每当此时，我或我的姐妹们就用儿童雪橇把他拉过纽约布鲁克林区的街道，一直送他到地铁的入口处。一到那儿，他便手抓扶手一直走到底下的台阶时才放开手，因为那里通道的空气暖和些，地面上没有结冰。到了曼哈顿，地铁站就在他办公楼的地下一层，在我们到布鲁克林接他回家之前他无需再走出楼来。

如今每当我想起这些，我惊叹一个成年男子要经受这种屈辱和压力得需要多么大的勇气啊！叹服他竟然能够做到这一点，不带任何痛苦，没有丝毫抱怨。

他从不说自己可怜，也从不嫉妒别人的幸运和能力。他所期望的是人们"善良的心"，当他得到时，人家真的对他很好。

如今我已经长大成人，我明白了"善良的心"是评价人的恰当的标准，尽管我仍不很清楚它的确切涵义，但是我却知道我有缺乏善心的时候。

虽然许多活动父亲都参加不了，但他仍然设法以某种方式参与进来。当一个地方棒球队发现缺少一个领队时，他便作了领队。因为他是个棒球迷，有丰富的棒球知识，他过去常带我去埃比茨棒球场观看布鲁克林的鬼精灵队的比赛。他喜欢参加舞会和晚会，乐意坐着看。

记得在一次海边晚会上，有人打架，动了拳头，推推搡搡。他不甘于坐在那里当观众，但又无法在松软的沙滩上自己站起来。于是，失望之下，他吼了起来："谁想坐下和我打？"没有人响应。但是第二天，人们都取笑他说比赛还没开始，拳击手就被劝认输，这还是头一次看见。

现在我知道一些事情他是通过我——他唯一的儿子来做的。当我打球时（尽管我打得很差），他也在"打球"。当我参加海军时，他也"参加"。当时我回家休息时，他一定要让我去他的办公室，在介绍我时，他说，"这是我儿子，但也是我自己，假如我不是这样的话，我也会去参军的。"

父亲离开我们已经很多年了，但是我时常想起他。我不知道他是否意识到我曾经不愿意让人看到和他走在一起的心理。假如他知道这一切，我很抱歉，因为我从没告诉过他我是多么愧疚、多么不孝、多么悔恨。每当我为一些琐事而抱怨时，为别人的好运而妒忌时，为我自己缺乏"善心"时，我就会想起我的父亲。

Practising
& Exercise

核心单词

embarrassed [im'bærəstli] *adj.* 窘的，尴尬的

halting ['hɔːltiŋ] *adj.* 跛的；蹒跚的

sleigh [slei] *n.* (轻便)雪橇

indignity [in'digniti] *n.* 轻蔑，屈辱；无礼举动

precisely [pri'saisli] *adv.* 精确地，准确地

frustration [frʌs'treiʃ ən] *n.* 挫折，失败，挫败

aloud [ə'laud] *adv.* 出声地；大声地

trifle ['traifl] *n.* 小事，琐事

实用句型

He never talked about himself as an object of pity，nor did he show any envy of the more fortunate or able.

他从不说自己可怜，也从不嫉妒别人的幸运和能力。

① nor 用在 never 之后表"也不"，用在句首时句子需倒装。

② talk about 谈论，谈到，类似的表达还有 talk with 与...交谈；talk of 谈论，谈到等固定搭配。

翻译行不行

1. 他帮助我度过了难关。(pull through)

....

2. 多少人参加了开业典礼? (participate in)

....

3. 即使下雨，他也会准时到的。(even though)

....

The Blessed Dress
幸运的结婚礼服

• Sandy Williams •

I got an **engagement** ring for Christmas. My boyfriend and I had been dating for almost a year and both felt the time was right to join our lives together in holy matrimony.

The month of January was spent planning our perfect Alabama June wedding. My mother, two sisters and I went to Huntsville, the closest town with a selection of bridal shops, to buy the gown that would play the leading role on my special occasion.

We had a wonderful time just being together and sharing silly jokes, but the day soon turned serious by afternoon: still no sign of the dress of my dreams. Both sisters were ready to give up and try another day in another town, but I **coerced** them into one more boutique.

I had a good feeling as we entered the quaint little shop filled with the scent of fresh flowers. The elderly clerk showed us several beautiful gowns in my size and price range, but none were right. As I opened the door to leave, the desperate shop owner announced she had one more dress in the back that was expensive and not even my size, but perhaps I might want to look at it anyway. When she brought it out, I squealed in delight.

This was it!

I rushed to the dressing room and slipped it on. Even though it was at least two sizes too large and more costly than I had anticipated, I talked Mom into buying it. The shop was so small it didn't offer alterations, but my excitement assured me I would be able to get it resized in my hometown.

Excitement wasn't enough. On Monday morning, my world crumbled when the local sewing shop informed me the dress simply could not be altered because of numerous hand-sewn pearls and sequins on the bodice. I called the boutique for suggestions but only got their answering machine.

A friend gave me the number of a lady across town who worked at home doing alterations. I was desperate and willing to try anything, so I decided to give her a call.

When I arrived at her modest white house on the outskirts of town, she carefully inspected my dress and asked me to try it on. She put a handful of pins into the shoulders and sides of my gown and told me to pick it up in two days. She was the answer to my prayers.

When the time came to pick it up, however, I grew skeptical. How could I have been so foolish as to just leave a $1,200 wedding dress in the hands of someone I barely knew? What if she made a mess out of it? I had no idea if she could even sew on a button.

Thank goodness my fears were all for naught. The dress still looked exactly the same, but it now fit as if it had been made especially for me. I thanked the cheerful lady and paid her modest fee.

One small problem solved just in time for a bigger one to emerge. On Valentine's Day, my fiance called.

"Sandy, I've come to the decision that I'm not ready to get married," he announced, none too gently. "I want to travel and experience life for a few years before settling down."

He apologized for the inconvenience of leaving all the wedding cancellations to me and then quickly left town.

My world turned upside down. I was angry and heartbroken and had no idea how to recover. But days flew into weeks and weeks blended into months. I survived.

One day in the fall of the same year, while standing in line at the supermarket, I heard someone calling my name. I turned around to see the alterations lady. She politely inquired about my wedding, and was shocked to discover it had been called off, but agreed it was probably for the best.

I thanked her again for adjusting my wedding gown, and **assured** her it was safely bagged and awaiting the day I would wear it down the aisle on the arm of my real "Mister Right". With a sparkle in her eye, she began telling me about her single son, Tim. Even though I wasn't interested in dating again, I let her talk me into meeting him.

I did have my summer wedding after all, only a year later. And I did get to wear the dress of my dreams—standing beside Tim, the man I have shared the last eighteen years of my life with, whom I would never have met without that **special** wedding gown.

桑迪·威廉姆斯

圣诞节的时候我订婚了。我和男友交往已快一年了，我们都感到是携手步入神圣的婚姻殿堂的时候了。

整个1月我都忙于准备我们6月将在阿拉巴马州举行的婚礼。我和母亲，连同两个姐姐前往最近的城市汉斯维尔的一些新娘服装店去挑选结婚礼服，这可是婚礼中至关重要的一个环节。

我们母女四人高高兴兴，有说有笑。但是到了下午，仍然没有看到我梦想中的结婚礼服。大家都有点不耐烦，我的两个姐姐都已经准备就此打道回府，改天再到其他的城镇去看看了，但是我硬拉她们陪我再多看一家小店。

当我们进入这家满是鲜花的精致小店时，我有一种很好的预感。上了年纪的店员给我们介绍了几件适合我穿的美丽礼服，价格也都在我的预算之内，但都不是我想要的。正当我打开店门准备离开时，孤注一掷的老板娘喊着，在后面仓库里还有一件礼服，这件礼服很贵，甚至没有我穿的号码，但是也许我会看一眼。当她拿出来时，我欣喜地叫出声来：

"就是这一件了！"

我冲进试衣间把身体滑进去。尽管它至少要大上两码，价格也比我预想的要高很多，但我仍说服母亲买下了它。这家店很小，连改衣服的服务都不提供，但是在激动之余，我确信能在我们家附近的裁缝店把它改好。

然而盲目的激动是无济于事的。礼拜一早上，当我们那儿的裁缝师告诉我因为礼服上手缝的珠子和饰片太多而没法改动时，我傻眼了。我打电话给那家服装店寻求建议，听到的却只是机器的自动应答。

一个朋友给了我一个镇上裁缝的电话，这个裁缝在家里干活。在绝望之余，我愿意进行任何尝试。于是我决定给她打个电话。

当我赶到她在城镇郊区的简陋的白色房子里时，她仔细地察看了我的礼服，并让我穿上看看。她用别针将礼服的肩膀处和两侧别上，让我两天后来取衣服。她正是我祈祷的福音。

该去取衣服了，我却忐忑不安起来。我怎么这么愚蠢，将一件价值 1 200 美元的礼服交到一个一点儿也不了解的人手里。如果她改坏了怎么办？我甚至不知道她会不会缝扣子。

谢天谢地，我的担心都是多余的。礼服仍跟以前一样，不过现在我穿上正合适，仿佛是为我量身定做的一样。我谢过那个高兴的女裁缝，并多付了些钱。

然而这只是解决了一个小问题，更大的问题还在后面。情人节那天，未婚夫打来了电话。

"桑迪，我决定了，我对婚姻还没有做好准备，"他说着，语气一点也不温柔，"在成家之前，我要到各处走走，享受几年单身生活。"

他把取消婚礼的所有麻烦留给我，然后很快离开了这个城镇。

我的世界被颠覆了。我愤怒，心碎，不知道该如何撑过去。然而随着日子一天天、一月月流走，我熬过来了。

这个秋季的一天，在超市排队结账的时候，我听见有人叫我的名字。一扭头，看到是那个女裁缝。她很有礼貌地问起我的婚礼，当得知被取消了时她非常惊讶，但随后告诉我下一个也许是最好的。

我再一次感谢她成功修改了我的结婚礼服，并向她保证，礼服被我安全地放起来了，等待着穿上它挽着我真正的"白马王子"走上红地毯的一天。她的眼睛里闪过亮光，开始跟我谈起她的单身儿子Tim。尽管我对重新约会没有兴趣，我还是听任她给我安排跟她儿子的约会。

我的夏季婚礼最终成为了现实，只不过是在一年以后。站在Tim身旁，我终于穿上了我梦中的结婚礼服。在随后的18年里，我们相亲相爱，相濡以沫。如果不是因为这件特殊的礼服，我们永远不会相遇。

核心单词

engagement [in'geidʒmənt] *n.* 订婚；婚约

coerce [kəu'əːs] *v.* 强制；迫使

anticipate [æn'tisipeit] *v.* 预期，期望；预料

crumble ['krʌmbl] *v.* 粉碎，弄碎

skeptical ['skeptikəl] *adj.* 怀疑的，多疑的

exactly [ig'zæktli] *adv.* 确切地，精确地；完全地

assured [ə'ʃuəd] *adj.* 确定的；自信的；确信的

special ['speʃəl] *adj.* 特殊的；专门的，专用的

实用句型

I did have my summer wedding after all，only a year later.

我的夏季婚礼最终成为现实，只不过是一年以后。

①did 在这里表示强调。

②later 是 late 的比较级，类似的表达还有 earlier-early 等。

翻译行不行

1. 快穿上衣服跟我来。(slip on)

....

2. 工作结束后请把工具收拾好。(pick up)

....

3. 他的提议被拒绝了。(turn down)

....

When Love Was the Adventure
爱的艰程

• Patrick •

On a cold January morning in 1936, George V was given a king's burial. Following his coffin was his eldest son, the handsome, much loved, Prince of Wales. He was about to be **proclaimed** the next king of England. He was that exceptional thing: a model royal. He was at ease in every company. Everyone expected him to shake the stuffiness out of the monarchy. But as time passed, as he span between the royal duties, people began to remark that the prince was approaching 40 and still unmarried. Only a privileged few knew that he'd been stepping out with the mysterious American, a woman who was cheating on her husband with the future king of England. This was the lady known as Wallis Simpson, whom he was determined to marry.

So now he was king, but no one could **persuade** him to give up Wallis. Not even Prime Minister Stanley Baldwin who spoke for the nation when he said Britain did not want an American divorcee for a queen. Ministerial car shuttled between Westminster and Buckingham Palace but the king could not be budged. He was forced to **abdicate** and all over the country flags flew at half-mast.

In the summer of 1937, there was a quiet wedding in France. The couple looked a bit nervous, especially the groom, but only a year before he'd been a king. Now he and his wife would be called the Duke and Duchess of Windsor.

So now the man who'd given up a kingdom and a woman who'd given up two husbands embarked on their endless round of fun and gaiety. In the war years they'd been trapped in the Bahamas, but **emerged** every now and then to attend the great cultural festivals where they startled the locals with the brilliance of their attire. But the man who'd been a king found he was now only a celebrity. *There were even rumors that he and the duchess were breaking up so they had to parade their devotion for the cameras.*

Four years later, it was the nation's turn to **mourn** the Duke and to reflect on one man's decision to trade the crown of England for the love of Wallis and the price they had both had to pay.

帕特里克

1936 年 1 月的一个寒冷的早晨，英国王室为乔治五世举行了国葬。跟在他灵柩后面的是他的长子——英俊而深受爱戴的威尔士王子。他将被宣布成为英国的新国王。他是个模范的皇室成员，卓尔不群又平易近人。人人都期望着他会一改王室拘谨沉闷的形象。但随着时间的流逝，在他履行王室职责的同时，人们开始注意到王子已年近 40 却仍然形只影单。只有少数几人知道他一直在和一位神秘的美国女子约会，她瞒着丈夫和未来的英国国王来往。这位女士就是沃丽斯·辛普森，是王子决意要娶的人。

他是国王，没人能说服他放弃沃丽斯。连首相斯坦利·巴尔德温也不行——他代表国家说英国不想让一个离过婚的美国人成为王后。大臣们的汽车在威斯敏斯特教堂和白金汉宫之间穿梭往返，但国王却丝毫不为之所动。他被迫让位，为此举国降下半旗。

1937年的夏天，他们静静地在法国举办了婚礼。两人看起来有点紧张，尤其是新郎，一年之前他还是个国王。但现在他和妻子被称为温莎公爵伉俪。

放弃了江山的他和曾经两度离婚的她开始去尽情地享乐。战争时代他们被困在巴哈马群岛，但偶尔会出席一些盛大的文化节庆，他们的华衣美服让当地人惊叹不已。不过曾为国君的他发现自己现在只是个名人。甚至有传言说他和公爵夫人将要离异，于是他们不得不在镜头前展现恩爱的一面。

四年后，全国哀悼公爵的逝世并深思他的抉择——他为了对沃丽斯的爱情放弃了英国王位，他们两人都为此付出了代价。

Practising

& Exercise

核心单词

proclaim [prə'kleim] v. 宣告；公布；声明

persuade [pə'sweid] v. 说服，劝服

abdicate ['æbdikeit] v. 正式放弃 (权力等)；退 (位)；辞 (职)

emerge [i'mə:dʒ] v. 浮现；出现

mourn [mɔ:n] v. 哀痛，哀悼

实用句型

There were even rumors that he and the duchess were breaking up so they had to parade their devotion for the cameras. 甚至有传言说他和公爵夫人将要离异，于是他们不得不在镜头前表现恩爱一面。

① 这是由 that 引导的同位语从句，同位语从句是对先行词的解释、补充和说明。

② break up 分离，类似的表达还有 break down 失败，故障；break into 闯入，打断；break out 爆发，突然发生等固定搭配。

翻译行不行

1. 他装出一副安详自若的样子。(at ease)

....

2. 他们又着手开始一项新的冒险。(embark on)

....

3. 我一直在考虑这件事。(reflect on)

....

An Ingenious Love Letter
一封绝妙的情书

• Richard •

There once lived a lad who was deeply in love with a girl, but disliked by the girl's father, who didn't want to see any further development of their love. The lad was eager to write to the girl, yet he was quite sure that the father would read it first. So he wrote such a letter to the girl:

My love for you I once **expressed**

no longer lasts, instead, my distaste for you

is growing with each passing day. Next time I see you,

I even won't like that look of yours.

I'll do nothing but

look away from you. You can never expect I'll

marry you. The last **chat** we had

was so dull and dry that you shouldn't think it

made me eager to see you again. If we get married, I **firmly**

believe I'll

live a hard life, I can never

live happily with you, I'll devote myself

but not

to you. No one else is more

harsh and selfish and less

solicitous and considerate than you.

I sincerely want to let you know

what I said is true. Please do me a favor by

ending our relations and refrain from

writing me a reply. Your letter is always full of

things which displease me. You have no

sincere care for me. So long! Please believe

I don't love you any longer. Don't think

I still have a love of you!

Having read the letter, the father felt relieved and gave it to his daughter with a light heart.

The girl also felt quite pleased after she read it carefully, her lad still had a deep love for her.

Do you know why? In fact, she felt very sad when she read the letter for the first time. But she read it for a few more times and, at last, she found the **key**—only every other line should be read, that is the first line, the third, the fifth...and so on to the end.

理查德

一个小伙子非常爱一位姑娘，但姑娘的父亲却不喜欢他，也不允许他们的爱情再发展下去。小伙子很想给姑娘写封情书，然而他知道姑娘的父亲会先看，于是他给姑娘写了这样一封信：

我对你表达过的爱

已经消逝。我对你的厌恶

与日俱增。当我看到你时

我甚至不喜欢你的那副样子。

我想做的一件事就是

把目光移往别处，我永远不会

和你结婚。我们最近的一次谈话

枯燥乏味，你别想

使我渴望再与你相见。假如我们结婚，我深信我将

生活得非常艰难，我也无法

快乐地和你生活在一起，我要把我的心

奉献出来，但绝不是

奉献给你。没有人能比你更

苛求和自私，所有人都比你更

关心我帮助我。

我诚挚地要你明白，

我讲的是真话，请你助我一臂之力

结束我们之间的关系，别试图

答复此信，你的信充满着

使我乏味的事情，你没有

对我的真诚关心。再见，请相信

我并不喜欢你，请你不要以为

我仍然爱着你！

姑娘的父亲看了这封信以后，很轻松，并高兴地把信给了姑娘。

姑娘在仔细看完信后也非常高兴，小伙子依然爱着她。

你知道她为什么高兴吗？其实，她初读时非常地忧伤。但是，在她又默读了几遍之后终于明白这封信的读法了。只读一、三、五行以此类推，直到信的结尾。

Practising
& Exercise

实战
提升篇

核心单词

express [iks'pres] *v.* 表达，陈述；表示

chat [tʃæt] *v.* 闲谈，聊天

firmly ['fɜːmli] *adv.* 坚固地；稳固地

solicitous [sə□'lisitəs] *adj.* 热心的；挂念的

sincere [sin'siə] *adj.* 衷心的，真诚的

key [kiː] *n.* 关键，要害

实用句型

Having read the letter, the father felt relieved and gave it to his daughter with a light heart.

姑娘的父亲看了这封信以后，很轻松，并高兴地把信给了姑娘。

①现在分词 having 在这里作状语。

② with a light heart 心情愉快地，另外还有，to one's heart's content 痛快吧，尽情地等。

翻译行不行

1. 请勿给动物喂食。(refrain from)

....

2. 事实上，我对绘画并不感兴趣。(in fact)

....

3. 那调皮的孩子终于睡着了。(at last)

....

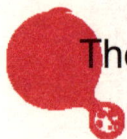

The Little Words That Work Marriage Magic
创造婚姻奇迹的小字眼

· Spike ·

Using terms of endearment like honey or sweetheart from time to time is a small but important way to keep a marriage loving. These terms make the other person feel loved and special. There are some other words that can help make your spouse feel special and aware of how much you love and **appreciate** him.

"Thank You." We would not never thank a friend or co-worker for helping us out. But sometimes we forget to thank the person we love most: our **spouse**. All couples forget now and then to thank each other for all they do. *But thanking each other is a good habit to fall into because gratitude is necessary for the growth of love*. Knowing that their actions are appreciated makes a couple more giving toward each other, and the more you give to each other the more your love will grow.

"Please." Please, like thank you, is easy to forget to say, but it too is very important in a relationship. Because it is another way of letting your partner know you don't take him for granted and that his time and effort count.

"You are great." Do you know that this sentence can make

him feel good about himself all day? Now that you know how nice it makes him feel to be complimented, you should try to do it as often as you can. As an added **bonus**, he will begin paying compliments to you more often. This is not surprising since, experts say, compliments are a two-way street. So the more compliments you give, the more you get. Often couples will think nice things about each other but not **verbalize** their thoughts because they're just not in the habit of doing so. But when one of them starts, the other will pick up on the **cue** and begin doing the same.

"I love you." in a new way, a small variation such as "I love you more each day" can make a big difference in how you feel about each other. When you say "I love you" the exact same way over and over, your spouse may start to **discount** it. On the other hand, a fresh phrase can help keep the relationship fresh. For instance, you can expressed your love for him by saying "I'm so glad you're in my life." I'm sure he will be really **impressed** and touched, and you two will feel closer.

斯帕克

经常用"宝贝"、"甜心"之类亲昵语，是婚姻永葆鲜活的一种小但很重要的方法。这些亲昵的词语能让人深切感受到对方的爱意，也能感受到自己在其心中的特殊地位。另外也有一些字眼能让爱人体会到自己在你心中的重要分量，感到你有多么爱他，多么欣赏他。

　　"谢谢你。"我们总会在朋友或同事的帮忙后表示感谢。然而，有时候却忘了感谢我们最爱的人。夫妻间时而会忘记彼此道谢，但这却是一个良好的习惯，在爱的成长路途中，是不可缺少的。只有自己所做的得到了对方的认同和欣赏，才会乐意给予更多。彼此给予的越多，爱就会增值越多。

　　"请"和**"谢谢"**一样容易被忽略，但这个字眼，在夫妻关系中，也是相当地有分量。因为它也能让你的爱人意识到，你并没有把他所做的事看做是理所当然的，他所付出的时间和努力是值得的。

　　"你真好。"你可知道，这句话能让他愉快一整天。既然你知道令爱人感受褒扬是很不错的，那么，你就应尽可能地这样对他说。这样做还有一个好处，就是他也会频繁地赞赏你。专家们认为，赞赏是条双向街。因而夫妻间的这种互赞效应也就不足为奇了。因为，你对爱人称赞得越多，你获得的赞扬也就越多。通常，夫妻彼此间都有好感，只是没养成习惯，故而没在言语上表达出来。只要其中一方开了口，另一方便会领会其意，如此效法。

　　"我爱你"的全新表达法，把"我爱你"稍加改动成"每天爱你多一点"，这样能使夫妻的感情生活大有改观。一遍遍地重复着"我爱你"，爱人可能就会对此不以为然了。不仅如此，一种新的表达能让夫妻关系时刻都有新鲜感。比如，要表达对他的爱意，你可以这样说，"我真高兴我的生命中有你"。我确信，他定会被深深地感动，于是，两颗心更近了。

Practising

& Exercise

实战
提升篇

核心单词

appreciate [ə'pri:ʃieit] v. 欣赏，感谢，感激

spouse [spauz] n. 配偶

bonus ['bəunəs] n. 奖金；额外津贴；特别补助

verbalize ['və:bəlaiz] v. 以言语表述；唠叨

cue [kju:] n. 提示；信号；线索

discount ['diskaunt] n. 折扣；打折扣

impress [im'pres] v. 给……极深的印象；使感动；使铭记

实用句型

But thanking each other is a good habit to fall into because gratitude is necessary for the growth of love. 夫妻间时而会忘记彼此道谢，但这却是一个良好的习惯，在爱的成长路途中，是不可缺少的。

①动名词 thanking 在这里作主语。

②fall into 形成，类似的表达还有 fall off(数量)减少；fall out 发生；fall down 失败等固定搭配。

翻译行不行

1. 朋友们偶尔聚会，畅谈学生时代的美好时光。(now and then)

....

2. 有些人常常对谣言信以为真。(take...for granted)

....

3. 像兔和鹿这样的动物整个冬天都是很活跃的，它们到处寻找食物。(such as)

....

The Furthest Distance in the World
世界上最遥远的距离

· Steven ·

The **furthest** distance in the world is not between life and
death
But when I stand in front of you
Yet you don't know that I love you

*The furthest distance in the world is not when I stand in
front of you*
Yet you can't see my love
But when **undoubtedly** knowing the love from both
Yet cannot be together

The furthest distance in the world is not being apart while
being in love
But when **plainly** can not resist the **yearning**
Yet pretending you have never been in my heart

The furthest distance in the world is not when plainly can not
resist the yearning
Yet pretending you have never been in my heart
But using one's indifferent heart
to **dig** an uncrossable river for the one who loves you

世界上最遥远的距离
不是生与死
而是我就站在你的面前
你却不知道我爱你

世界上最遥远的距离
不是我站在你面前
你却不知道我爱你
而是明明知道彼此相爱
却不能在一起

世界上最遥远的距离
不是明明知道彼此相爱
却不能在一起
而是明明无法抵挡这股想念
却还得故意装作丝毫没有把你放在心里

世界上最遥远的距离
不是明明无法抵挡这股想念
却还得故意装作丝毫没有把你放在心里
而是用自己冷漠的心
为爱你的人挖掘了一条无法跨越的沟渠

I wish someone were waiting for me somewhere

我希望有人在什么地方等我

Practising

& Exercise

核心单词

furthest ['fə:ðist] *adj.* 最大程度的；最远的；极远的

undoubtedly [ʌn'dautidli] *adv.* 毫无疑问地；肯定地

plainly ['pleinli] *adv.* 清楚地，明显地

yearning ['jə:niŋ] *n.* 思念；渴望

dig [dig] *v.* 掘（土）；挖（洞，沟等）；掘取

实用句型

The furthest distance in the world is not when I stand in front of you，yet you don't know that I love you. 世界上最遥远的距离，不是我站在你面前，你却不知道我爱你。

① furthest 是 far 的最高级形式，另一形式为 farthest。

②in front of 在 ... 的前面，类似的表达还有 in the front of 在 ... 的前部等。

翻译行不行

1. 该国无力抵抗侵略。(resist)

....

2. 我不会自命为学者。(pretend)

....

3. 你去也好，不去也好，我都无所谓。(indifferent)

....